Be Intentional No Matter What

By

Toledo Lopez

Be Intentional No Matter What
Copyright © 2021 Toledo Lopez
All rights reserved.
No portion of this publication may be reproduced, stored in any electronic system, or transmitted in any form or by any means without the written permission from the author. Brief quotations may be used in literary reviews.

ISBN-13: 978-1-7360431-3-4
Library of Congress Control Number: 2021900960

Dedication

TK and KD thanks for empowering me with love, strength and wisdom. I am a better person because of you. I absolutely cherish my role as your Mom.

Table of Contents

DEDICATION 1

FOREWORD 3

SURVIVAL MODE 8

FINANCES 20

QUESTION THE METHOD BUT NEVER THE MOTIVE 25

THE ART OF SACRIFICE 32

UNWAVERING FAITH 41

OVERCOMING MINDSET 44

THE GREATEST INVESTMENT 54

MIND BATTLES: THE LAW OF ATTRACTION 62

THE LAW OF ENERGY 67

FAIL YOUR WAY TO SUCCESS 74

THE GREATEST OF THESE 79

YOUR PRESENCE – THEIR EXPOSURE 83

BE INTENTIONAL NO MATTER WHAT 89

HEART TO HEART INTERVIEWS 95

SELAH INSPIRATION RESOURCES 127

66 DAY CHALLENGE 130

ACKNOWLEDGEMENTS 142

REFERENCES 151

ABOUT THE AUTHOR 152

FOREWORD

Much of what we invest, sacrifice and secretly deal with is never truly known by anyone other than ourselves. Many will witness us go through our personal journey, but few will understand the profound lessons hidden behind the situations we encounter. The more challenging and perplexing the situations, the more significant the underlying lessons are to our growth. These lessons provide the wisdom and inspiration to discovering our unique purpose in life.

An obvious digression to this discovery is ensuring our mind is focused on what really matters. So often we put all of our energy into what is going wrong in our lives instead of focusing on what we should be learning about ourselves while facing challenges. Life is harsh and this harshness can distract us from progressing and operating at our full potential. I have literally said to myself after going through a challenging situation, "Look at how much time I wasted doing absolutely nothing productive because I was so focused on my feelings being hurt or someone doing something I did not like." The older I get the more I realize life is too short to allow anything or anyone to distract me from living the life I deserve. I am reminded of a story I heard about a little boy who enjoyed eating candy. One day the little boy was sitting on his front porch after school eating his candy just as fast as he could open the wrappers. A woman passing by witnessed how fast the little boy was eating the candy. She said all that candy is not good for you and might spoil your dinner. The little boy said I don't know about that but my grandpa lived to be a 102. The woman said, "Wow! You mean by eating candy?" The little boy said, "No, by minding his own business." This little boy had the right mindset. Do not let others or situations distract you from focusing on your purpose.

This takes work and is a process we must perfect over time. The key is realizing the power of our minds. In life we have two options in how we want to live. When we fill our minds with positive thoughts, we start creating, inventing and experiencing a change for the better. If we fill our minds with negative thoughts, we stagnate our growth. It is hard for the mind to formulate a better way if we decide to allow negative thoughts to fester. Scientists say the brain is arguably the most powerful organ in the human body. Think about what happens when you attempt to stand up from your chair. Your brain sends signals to your leg muscles and you literally thing about standing up before you stand. So, why is it so hard for you to believe your thoughts can revolutionize or destroy your life. What we allow to fester in our minds impacts our emotions and will eventually manifest in our behaviors.

"Finally, brethren, whatsoever things are true, whatsoever things are honest, whatsoever things are just, whatsoever things are pure, whatsoever things are lovely, whatsoever things are of good report; if there be any virtue, and if there be any praise, think on these things" (Philippians 4:8). Protecting our mind is the most important practice we can incorporate into our lives. Yes, it is a practice that must be intentionally carried out every single second. People will say and do things to make you think less of yourself or you may think negative thoughts, but you have to fight against those thoughts. The fight should look more proactive than reactive. We all encounter situations that trigger negative thoughts, but how we deal with those thoughts is the key. As stated earlier, the mind is so powerful and what you allow to fester in your mind will ultimately manifest itself through the decisions and actions you make. Most battles are won or lost in your mind. So, it is important to remember whose and who you are. Understand that you have the power to control your mind and prepare against the negativity seeking to hold you down or derail you from your God-given destiny. Winning this battle will equip you to not only help yourself but will also give you the stamina and tools to help others.

As a single parent this reality is magnified to another level. Who imagines a life fashioned with being responsible for making every decision concerning one's children, robbing Peter to pay Paul, putting his/her life on hold, struggling to make ends meet and/or feeling guilty about their children having to deal with a broken family. I cannot think of a young boy or girl who dreams of becoming a single parent. I am sure many have faced this challenge or something worse. They feel like this is the only life is possible for them. Not so! There is so much more to life than the unrelenting challenges. In life you will have trials and tribulations, but the key is how you show up while going through the trials and tribulations. My story as a single parent is intended to inspire and inform others how to be intentional in living their desired life despite their current predicament.

If you ordered this book expecting some succulent timeline of events surrounding my divorce and how awful the other parent was to my children and I, you are going to be highly disappointed. I am convinced that I endured this single parent journey to inspire others to work through challenges positively. This is key as it frees our minds to have a more optimistic outlook on life. When we allow anything or anyone to make us feel hurt, angry or unworthy, then we give our power over to that thing or person. It is impossible to evolve into the person you are destined to become if someone else has the power. Whose standards are you rising to? Instead of focusing on the negative, we must work to embrace every experience as an opportunity to grow into a better person. When we realize the challenges we are facing do not define us and get over feelings we naturally start evolving into our greatness. Embrace your journey and resolve within yourself what is required to bring forth the best version of yourself.

I realized my two innocent children deserved the best life and it was my responsibility to provide an environment that would promote positivity, love, uniqueness, growth and greatness. This was essential if they were going to reach their full potential. I intentionally decided I was going to get over my trauma as quickly as possible and, at a very minimum, positively work through my issues. I wanted my children to have a fighting chance at living their best lives. Whether we decide our energy will be positive or negative, there is a high probability that energy is going to transfer to those around us. Energy is contagious and determines our potential for growth. It will even cause others to have a negative or positive experience in their lives. If our desire is to live our best life and see others discover their greatness, we must train our thoughts, words and actions to remain positive no matter what. This is no small feat but is imperative. It will take a lot of intentional work, but we must stay focused on improving ourselves, relationships, finances, health and overall outlook on life. We must believe the power lies within us to live the life we desire and deserve.

SURVIVAL MODE

Selah: For I know the thoughts that I think toward you saith the Lord, thoughts of peace, and not of evil, to give you an expected end. Jeremiah 29:11

As I ponder over my life, I cannot help but ask myself, Who would have ever thought that I would be raising two boys by myself in my early thirties? How did I make it through these years all by myself? Even more importantly I asked, How can my story inspire single Moms, single Dads and those supporting them? At the age of thirty-two, I was divorced with two amazing young boys to raise and I was scared out of my mind. I realized I was not the first single Mom, but I was still frightened. I felt alone amongst those mentioned in the following research conducted in the United States. (References for all research are sited in the References section).

- A new Pew Research Center study of 130 countries and territories shows that the U.S. has the world's highest rate of children living in single-parent households.

- As of 2020, 18.99 million families in the U.S. were headed by a single parent.

- There were 15 million *single mother*-headed households in the United States in 2019. 25% of U.S. families are headed by a *single parent,* and 80% of *single-parent* headed households are moms — or 21% of children live primarily with a *single mother*.

- 1.5 million children are living in a single-parent household because of the death of one parent. (Owens)

- Two-thirds (66%) said that more single women having children was bad for society, and just 4% said this trend was good for society (the remaining 29% said the trend doesn't make much difference). At the same time, about half (48%) said more unmarried couples raising children was bad for society, while just 6% said it was good for society and 45% said it didn't make much difference.

- 53% of whites viewed more unmarried couples raising children as a bad thing, compared with 37% of blacks and 32% of Hispanics.

- Other data suggest there has been some softening in views towards unmarried parenthood. In 2012, 48% of adults agreed or strongly agreed that single parents could raise children as well as two parents can, according to the General Social Survey. This marked an increase from 1994, when just 35% said as much. At the same time, the share of people who disagreed or strongly disagreed that single parents could raise children as well as two parents ticked down, from 48% to 41%.

- The overwhelming majority (83%) of Republicans and independents who lean to the Republican Party said that more single women having children without a partner is bad for society; 56% of Democrats and those who lean Democratic said the same. Partisan differences were even wider on attitudes about unmarried parents raising children together: While 70% of Republicans saw this as bad for society, about half as many Democrats (32%) said the same.

2019

(in 1,000s)

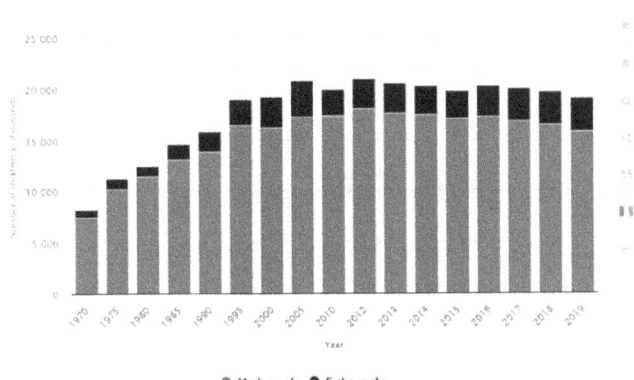

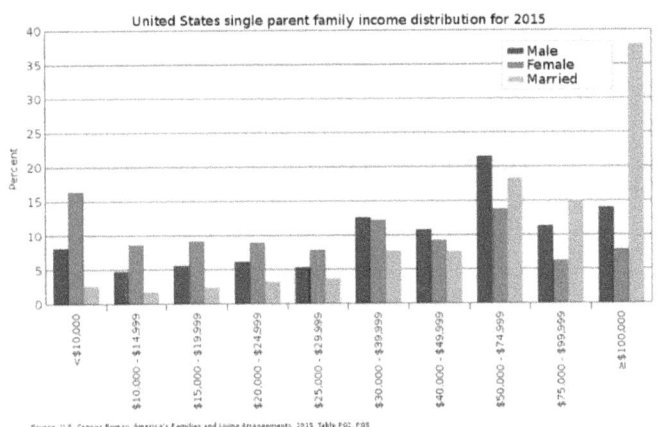

Share of unmarried parents who are dads has more than doubled

% of unmarried parents who are ...

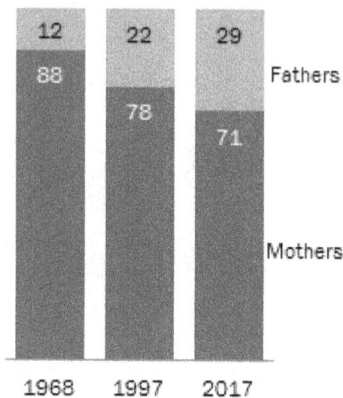

About one-fourth of solo parents are poor

% living in poverty, by parent type

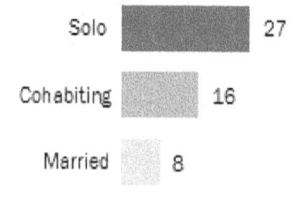

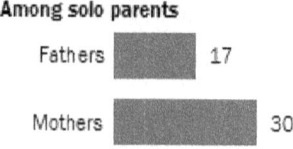

Majority viewed more solo moms as bad for society in 2015

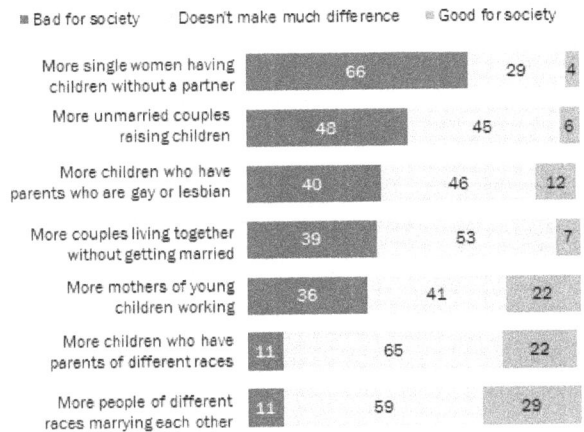

In 2015, Republicans were twice as likely as Democrats to say more unmarried couples raising children are a 'bad thing' for society

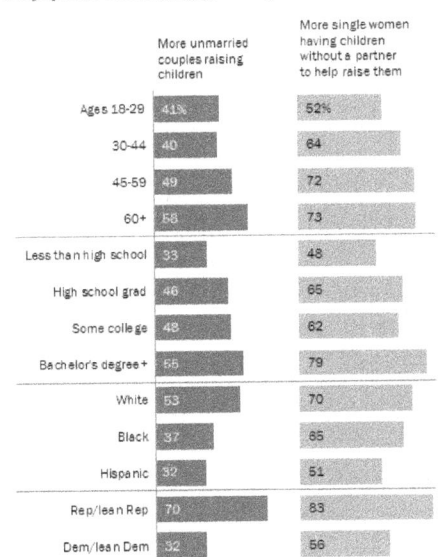

This prevalence is due in part to the growing trend of children born outside marriage — a societal trend that was virtually unheard of, decades ago. As a result, single parents are raising more than one-third of U.S. children as of 2019.

Single mothers are one of the poorest populations, many of them vulnerable to homelessness. In the United States, nearly half (45%) of single mothers and their children live below the poverty line, also referred to as the poverty threshold. They lack the financial resources to support their children when the birth father is unresponsive. *(United States Census Bureau 2015)*

Whether you start from day one as a single parent or become one due to divorce or death, understanding that life will transition is an understatement. Single parents experience countless moments of emotional roller coasters, learning curves, low self-esteem, guilt, vulnerability, poverty, fear, self-doubt, and unwarranted discrimination. These experiences undeniably create very difficult and traumatic moments that are hard to bounce back from. However, I am a living witness it is absolutely possible for single parents and their children to live quality and abundant lives while facing these unexpected challenges. Once largely limited to poor women and minorities, single motherhood is now becoming a new norm.

Facing these challenges all by myself was a reality I honestly was not ready to take on nor did I feel equipped to take on until I looked at my two innocent babies. They were eight and four years old and my heart was crushed to see them suffering. I knew I would be okay, but my babies would likely take a while to adjust to this new life of single parenthood.

With an aching heart I quickly switched to operating in survival mode. From the outside looking in, it appeared I was doing okay because at least I was making it. However, there were nights I did not eat dinner because I wanted to ensure my children had seconds and keeping gas in my car was a constant juggle. It was a very dark moment for me because I realized there was more to life than simply surviving.

When I decided it was time to stop playing the victim, my mentality changed from surviving to thriving. It was not an overnight process nor was it easy. I vowed never to play victim again and decided to work through my pain and frustration during my alone time. I would cry in the shower or cry in the bed until the pillows were soaked. My hard truth was accepting my poor decision and focusing on what really mattered. At the end of each day, I still had to figure out how to ensure my children were emotionally stable, how we were going to eat, where we were going to stay and how to provide clothes and shoes to wear. I could only focus on providing the bare necessities instead of thinking outside the box to create an abundant life for us. My desire was to thrive instead of merely surviving. As a result, I was determined to not complain or become bitter because of what I was experiencing. I put all my focus on:

1. Understanding my "why" in life. My children were my inspiration. They reminded me that we were meant to thrive. There were days I felt like the responsibility of raising the boys was insurmountable, but when I thought about their happiness, I instantly knew I was designed for this task. I knew no weapon formed against us would prosper.

2. Spending time with people who were already where I wanted to be spiritually, emotionally and financially.

3. Implementing strategies to improve my personal development.

I was determined that my children would not suffer due to my inability to get over my disappointment. Yes, I was devastated and hurt, but what did that have to do with the fact I was responsible for their well-being. I was very comfortable with nurturing and teaching my children but wondered how I was supposed to do everything else by myself. After my divorce, the reality of almost being homeless and wondering if my paycheck would make it until the end of the month was the pressure I needed. It was this type of uncertainty which pushed me to shift out of my comfort zone and seek ways to thrive. As a Mom who simply wanted the best for her children, I forced myself to become comfortable in the uncomfortable. My journey evolved into an experience that reinforced the importance of perseverance and resolve within myself. I decided to not give up and declared victory even though all I saw was defeat.

This experience reminded me of watching two peach trees grow that we planted a few years ago. During the fall season, we planted two peach pits close to each other, hoping to have peaches the following summer. They endured the drought and strong winds of the fall months, brittle cold weather of the winter months, the drenching rain of spring and the high temperatures of the summer to ultimately become strong peach trees. The trees had to experience each season to produce the fruit we desired. The growth of the peach trees did not magically happen overnight. We experience life just like the peach trees. We start out as a tiny seed, develop branches, grow leaves and eventually evolve into human beings full of greatness, but not before experiencing some or all the seasons of life. Regardless of the season we are experiencing, we still need water, food and sunshine to grow properly. It is a process that does not happen immediately. At times, life is overwhelming, but we must realize each experience encountered is valuable and intended to fortify us as we evolve into greatness. The trees did not produce fruit the following summer, but they weathered each season to grow strong and tall. The true merit of greatness is gracefully responding to what life presents and realizing we are born with everything we need to overcome. Life is about evolving into who we are destined to be in this world despite any situation.

This mentality was the foundation I needed to elevate my life. I started believing in myself and as a result gained favor and increased my finances to a six-digit enterprise in one year. During this bold transformation, I decided to overcome all obstacles no matter what. This inspired my goal to teach and help others navigate through their challenges in order to live a life of abundance. Life is about thriving vice merely surviving.

Here are five steps I followed to be intentional about thriving in life:

1. **Being Aware Of Triggers Causing Negative Thoughts.** If you recognize what bothers you, then you have a better chance of managing your emotions. I am not saying negative situations will not happen, but I am saying you will deal with the situations better.
2. **Recognizing Fear Is Irrational.** I remember a trip I took with a friend to Dubai. One night she came

running out of her hotel room because she saw a spider on her pillow. She knocked on my door, but I was in the shower. My friend sat outside her door until she could reach me. I was so amazed that she thought it was safer to sit outside her room in a strange country than to go back into her room and wait on the couch. Reaching our full potential in life requires us to recognize how irrational it would be to never attempt living our best life due to fear.

3. **Practice Self-Introspection.** I was a teacher in Okinawa, Japan about 20 years ago where I met one of my besties. The very first time I saw her I said, "She thinks she is cute with all that fake hair in her head." I walked in my classroom immediately after saying this, touched my head and said, "Wait a minute, I have fake hair on my head." I had to ask myself what I was dealing with internally to make such a negative comment about someone I had never met before. I realized at that moment I had some work to do. In fact, that lady and I became friends because she decided to help me overcome a very traumatic life event that happened not too long after I first saw her. Who would have helped me if I had kept that same negative mindset about her? That lady and I are still friends today and she is the reason my family and I had the opportunity to meet David Tyree. Yes, New York Giants number 85 who caught the ball on his helmet during the 2008 Superbowl to defeat the undefeated Patriots is now one of our family friends. The lady who thought she was cute with her fake hair is the sister of David Tyree. My life would not be as successful as it is today if Tara and I had never met.

4. **Denounce Negativity.** The only way to defeat negativity is to recognize it, understand what triggers

it and announce it. Announce you will not live a defeated life and declare you will have victory over every area of your life. After I had an honest conversation with myself, I realized Tara was not just cute, but she was drop dead gorgeous. I still do not understand jealousy between women, but I do know I almost missed the opportunity of having a loyal friend by my side for almost twenty years. And did I say I got to meet David Tyree? You must denounce negative thoughts in order to reach your destiny.

5. **Decide.** It is your decision and your decision alone to allow negativity to fester in your mind. Every day we make decisions on what to eat, wear and work. You should be as intentional about whether to allow negativity to impact you mind.

Thriving takes work and if you are serious about living your best life, reach out to my team at www.selahinspiration.com for additional tools and techniques uniquely designed to teach you how to be intentional no matter what. These resources are uniquely designed to teach you how to be intentional no matter what. We only have one life and it is very short. Do you want to merely survive or thrive?

Finances

Selah: A good [man] leaveth an inheritance to his children's children: and the wealth of the sinner [is] laid up for the just. Proverbs 13:22

As I navigated through this new journey, I am reminded of a conversation I had with an elderly woman who worked in my office. One morning at 6:00 a.m. she pounced into my office and without saying good morning, she asked, "Why on earth are you working before I arrive and why are you still here when I leave?" I was more stunned she noticed my time in the office than how she approached me. I had to decide at that moment to tell her the truth or act like I had a lot of work to do. I decided to be partially transparent and proceeded to tell her I was working overtime to pay off bills and hopefully get myself in a position to buy my own home. The whole truth would have been I needed the money for other things too, but buying the home was the driving force. The next day she came into my office and insisted that I tell her what kind of bills required this much time in the office. With more passion and concern than anyone, she asked, "You work anywhere from twelve to sixteen hours a day. What about your ex-husband? What about your family?" As I was thinking about her questions, I was unaware this lady had gone back to her desk, written a check for $10,000 and with tears in her eyes she said please take this to help you get your boys back in the type of home they are used to. I, of course said, "No", but she dropped the check on the desk and left the office. I had to leave too because her kindness overwhelmed me. I put the check in the bank and utilized it towards the purchase our new home.

I invested in our financial future by paying off my debts to purchase a new home. I firmly believe my internalization of the type of financial lifestyle I wanted for us attracted this lady to me. Other than God providing a miracle, who gives away $10,000? In 2010, I finally paid down my debt, saved and was able to purchase close to a half million-dollar home in Virginia. Things were great! The guys were ecstatic to be in our new home and both settled into the neighborhood well. They met new friends and stayed involved with the activities they enjoyed. I continued to work hard so they could have a great life.

Real Moms and Dads do whatever they need to do to provide and take care of their children. They rob Peter to pay Paul. Not Eat. Work multiple jobs. Get very little sleep. If absentee fathers or mothers are not actively involved and do not financially provide for their children then one parent faces an enormous challenge. Single parents cannot make the other parent spend time with the children but should make sure they give themselves and their children a fighting chance and file for alimony and child support. This is essential to your financial freedom and helps you build memories with your children. One day I decided I was no longer going to settle for the "rat race" and implemented a strategy to get out of debt. I used all my extra funds to aggressively pay off bills instead of getting a new car or new wardrobe. In less than a year, I was debt free! Here are the steps I put in place to accomplish this goal:

1. **Learned to say "No!" to kids, family and friends:** I had to realize my children did not have to have

everything they wanted. For some reason, after I bought our home in Northern Virginia, I wanted the boys to have a lot of material things. I did not realize I was only hurting the boys more than I was helping them. Sure, they were getting the latest X-Box game or new pair of shoes, but I was hindering my ability to help them by not saving for their future.

2. **Figured out my total debt and paid the highest interest rate bills down first**: I calculated all my debt down to the penny. This total included money I owed family/friends, credit card and personal loan companies. Once I figured out how much I owed, I started paying off one bill at a time.

3. **Saved 20% of income for the unexpected and leisure times**: I saved 20% of my income for unexpected and leisure time. The first category was for true emergencies like replacing a refrigerator, fixing the car or buying tires. The second category is set up to help pay for vacations, unexpected college expenses for my sons or buying new clothes.

4. **Developed a budget:** This has been a life saver and eye opener at the same time. Developing a budget gave me a good perspective on how much I was overspending and revealed how to save even more money. I quickly realized I did not need a new wardrobe every season and having every cable channel was not important. This perspective helped me get closer to my ultimate goal of saving more.

5. **Worked an extra job:** I have worked four jobs at one time to pay off debt, to simply get by and/or to save, and it was exhausting. Weigh the pros and cons of taking on a second job. Is it worth being away from

your children and the physical wear and tear on your body down?

6. **Saved 20% of income for retirement**: Single mothers are a growing part of the population. I realized after putting my first son through school, that prioritizing my retirement above my children's anticipated expenses was necessary for my children and I to succeed as a family.

7. **Created a Last Will and Testament (Will):** If you do not have a Will, please provide one quickly. If your children are over eighteen, have them create a Will too. This is simply to protect what you and your children have worked so hard to build as a family.

8. **Established a system to check my finances each week**: I spent ten minutes a day tracking my spending habits, expenses and net income. When I gained more control of my finances I only checked it weekly. This strategy worked for me. I encourage you to find a strategy which helps you track your finances.

I remember helping a friend who was in her early fifties. We will call her Lisa. Lisa was diagnosed with cancer. She could not work and as a result could no longer maintain her financial responsibilities. Lisa had always worked hard and lived life to the fullest. She never saw this coming. How could she be doing so great one day and the next day unable to even work? She fell behind on all her bills. Eventually Lisa foreclosed on her home and had to move in with family. This was not the optimal lifestyle Lisa dreamed of having in her fifties. She lost everything including her health. Lisa's situation really resonated with me the day I helped her clean out her home and move in with family. I started thinking about whether I was on the right financial track. I was devasted to see Lisa's predicament but grateful to gain this insight and wisdom in my late thirties. This motivated me to create an excel spreadsheet to track my finances. This eye-opener was a great visual of how I was tracking my expenditures and payments. Any excess income was used to invest and save.

My excel spreadsheet created the awareness I needed to ensure my financial stability and the legacy for my children. Please understand waiting until you are older to save or to secure your financial stability might not be the best option. Different responsibilities like helping an aging parent, unexpected health care expenses or providing for grandchildren could prevent you from having the lifestyle you desire.

If you are serious about tracking your finances and having ample resources for your desired lifestyle and legacy for you family, grab a copy of my "Income Legacy" spreadsheet from www.selahinspiration.com/shop. This spreadsheet put me on trajectory to saving six-digits in one-year versus living paycheck to paycheck.

Question the Method But Never the Motive

Selah: And these words, which I command thee this day, shall be in thine heart: And thou shalt teach them diligently unto thy children, and shalt talk of them when thou sittest in thine house, and when thou walkest by the way, and when thou liest down, and when thou risest up. Deuteronomy 6:6-7

If you are a parent and/or involved in the daily rearing of children, I know you are aware of all the mixed emotions that come with this responsibility. In some two-parent households, the responsibility of raising children is balanced out more and is not as stressful as a single-parent household. Both are manageable, but one undoubtably must switch to survivor mode because they feel neglected for the most part. Regardless of what situation or challenge a single parent faces there is always the misconception that they should have the strength and wisdom to handle whatever comes their way. Is it that no one cares enough to get involved? Is it out of sight/out of mind? This is a harass criticism but is indisputably and painfully true that single parents are overlooked and sometimes regarded as individuals with limited knowledge and wisdom on raising children.

Most single parents feel they are not allowed to show their vulnerabilities, not allowed to cry, not allowed to show distress and the list goes on. This inadvertently but distinctively creates two types of single parents:

> **1.** One will succumb to the mental distress this responsibility creates and will likely stop working at taking care of their responsibility.

> **2.** The other will experience the exact same emotion but find the strength from deep inside to make the decision that they are going to live the best life possible, no matter what happens. They accept the fact that the road may be challenging and they have to operate in survival mode. Under no circumstances will they stop working towards what they know their family deserves.

The latter parent understands there will be situations from one extreme to the next to deal with. Some days will be full of laughter and great memories of simply being in their children's presence. On the other end of the spectrum there will be days the only thing they know to do is pray. Figuring out how to deal with each child is a job within itself. You can have a child who does well in sports but struggles with simply turning assignments in on time Then another child who does well in school but needs help learning how to organize. I am still in amazement that two children can come from the same household but have a completely different mindset regarding life. The challenges, joys, uncertainty, and hurt created from parenting is sharper than a two-edged sword that pierces your very soul and spirit at times. It is truly the hardest job I have ever done but I figured out how to thrive as a parent using these basic principles:

1. Sacrifice – The act of giving up something that you want to keep especially in order to help someone else. It is imperative to give up your desires so your children have what they need. Sometimes this means you cannot get the next red bottom shoes because you must pay for Math tutoring. Or make sure you have enough gas in your car to take your child back and forth to Chinese lessons and football practice. What is best for them should always override what you desire and oftentimes what you need.

2. Faith – To have complete trust or confidence in someone or something. The mental strength you embody is imperative when raising children. Your children did not ask to be here, and they deserve the best that life can offer. When you are faced with challenges and obstacles, focus on the positive. Talking and thinking positive will not automatically change things for the better but will make life seem more manageable. As a result, you will be modeling and teaching your children how to handle unfortunate events that happen in their lives.

3. Investment – The action or process of investing money and time for profit or material result. When children express interest in certain dreams or if the parent, recognizes potential, they should do everything possible to nurture and support them in being successful. This is how First Lady Obama, Beyoncé, Elvis Presley and Kobe Bryant, became successful. It is that simple. If you see or hear of potential in your children, invest and nurture those gifts.

4. Love – Love *beareth all things, believeth all things, hopeth all things, endureth all things.* There is no love like a parent. A parent's love is so selfless and strong that life becomes no longer about you, but about your children. There should not be anything that anyone can do to make a parent inflict harm to their own children. I am reminded of a story where King Solomon revealed true feelings and relationships of two Mothers to a child they were fighting over. Two mothers living in the same house each with a son, but one son died. One of the babies had been smothered, and each mother claimed the remaining son as her own. Calling for a sword, Solomon declared his judgment: the baby would be cut in two, each woman to receive half. One mother did not contest the ruling, declaring that if she could not have the baby then neither of them could, but the other begged Solomon, "Give the baby to her, just don't kill him!" The king declared the second woman the true mother, as a mother would even give up her baby to someone else if that was necessary to save his life.

5. Presence – The state or fact of existing, occurring, or being present in a place or thing. Showing up for your children when they are doing great and when they are in trouble should look almost the same. As a parent, you must show up all the time – not just when it is convenient for you. Your children need to know that you support them regardless of what is going on with them.

6. Exposure – The act of being exposed to connect with something. I took my children to the library, to football camps, to visit colleges, on overseas trips, to concerts, to free plays, foreign language lessons, sewing classes, modeling and acting auditions, cello lessons, science & technical classes, mission trips to foreign countries. You should expose your children to as much as possible to help them figure out what they have an interest in and what they may want to pursue as they grow.

7. Greatness – The quality of being great, distinguished or eminent. Teach your children that no matter what challenges they face, that they are important and deserve the best. Whether your children experience the good or the bad, assist them in understanding what life lessons they should be learning from their experiences.

These principles remind me of the first single parent identified in the Bible. An Egyptian slave, Hagar, became a single parent due to Sarah insisting Hagar become a surrogate for her and Abraham. After the birth of Hagar's child, Sarah forced Hagar and the child to leave. God came to Hagar in her distress and let her know that He was with her. Single parents can learn from Hagar's experience. When she cried out to God, He drew near. Hagar called the Lord "the God who sees me." Despite how lonely single parenting may be at times, parents can take comfort in remembering that they are never alone. God promises to be a father to the fatherless and a defender of widows and orphans (Genesis 16 and Psalm 68:5).

The most important thing for any parent to remember is God created our children and has a plan for their lives. They were entrusted to us regardless of our family situation and their Creator expects us to take the responsibility to raise them in a godly manner. Single parents may find this more challenging than two parent households, but when they engage the help of others in Christ, their children can thrive. Jesus has a special tenderness for children and single parents can rest assured that He cares for their children. When single parents model loyalty, perseverance, love, purity, honor, and honesty before their children, they are earning the respect that will help those children emulate that behavior. As a single parent, you can rest in the promise that God's grace will fill in the gaps as He helps you raise your children. In fact, this concept can be incorporated with any challenge we face in life.

To make progress you must have a good understanding of where you are in life. What are your strengths and weaknesses? What are your goals? I have provided an exercise below known as the "Wheel of Life" or "Life Balance Wheel", which is one of the most powerful and visual tools you could use to increase your self-awareness. This activity will help you establish your unique foundation and provide a good perspective on what area/s should be prioritized for you to operate in your greatness and live a life of abundance in every area of your life.

How to Use the Wheel of Life (Instructions)

1. Review the eight categories on the Life Balance Wheel. If necessary, you can split or rename a category to add in something that is missing or make it more meaningful for you.
2. Rank your level of satisfaction with each area of your life by drawing a curved line across each segment (see

image for example). Scoring is between 1 (very dissatisfied) and 10 (fully satisfied). So, if it is helpful number the line starting from 0 back to 10.
3. The perimeter of the circle represents your "Wheel of Life". Now, look at your completed wheel and ask, "If this was your Wheel of Life, would it be the ride you want for the rest of your life?"
4. Identify at least one action to work on to improve your score in ONLY one area of the wheel – improving one area of your life will ignite the life balance and abundance you deserve.

TODAY'S DATE:

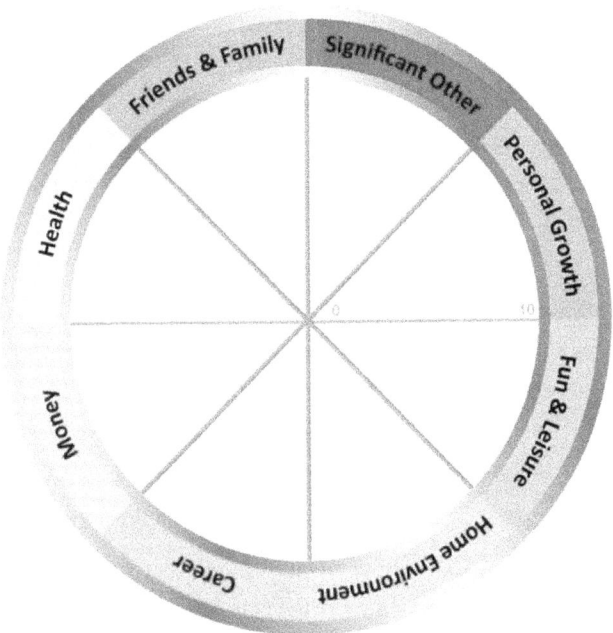

THE ART OF SACRIFICE

Selah: Be in a place where no weapon formed against you shall prosper – where everything meant to destroy you builds you up.

My Dad died when I was eight years old, and up until this point I was the typical happy, young girl. My father spent a lot of time with me. I remember spending Saturdays with him at the park, riding our bikes, washing the car or taking a ride with him on his motorcycle. At a very young age, I knew I was a princess and that my father loved me, unconditionally. I still remember where I was when he died. It was a beautiful spring day and I was at my grandmother's house playing in the yard. From a distance, I could hear the roaring of motorcycles approaching. I quickly ran to the end of the driveway and was so excited to see my dad leading the pack. I started waving like crazy hoping to stop my dad. I knew I could not go with him, but I just wanted to jump in his lap and hug him tight.

The pack of motorcycles roared by and I was so hurt, but soon got over it. I started back playing with my cousins and a few hours later my grandmother said she had something to tell me. Still playing, I asked my grandmother what was going on and that is when she shared the sad news with me. All I could see was a glare and I ran to a closet and hid until my Mother came to pick me and my siblings up. While I was in the closet, I did not cry initially. I was in total shock. Then I thought of all the great memories and laughs, and the warm tears stung my eyes and started flowing down my cheeks. I still do not remember leaving the closet. In fact, my next memory was seeing my dad at his funeral. The pain was so surreal that I honestly felt like I was sitting on that front row by myself.

I had a flashback of coming home one day, nearly in tears, after two boys who I thought were cute asked me, "Why do you walk so funny?" I had no idea that I was extremely pigeon toed and knocked kneed to the point that the doctors did not think I would be walking by the time I was sixteen. My dad asked why I was looking so sad and when I told him without even pausing, he said, "You are my princess, perfect in every way and there will only be one of you." The moment he said "princess", I was wrapped around his finger and knew I was perfectly fine. Now that he was gone, who was going to make me smile when I came home sad because of other kids picking on me? My world changed in that split second and quite frankly has never been the same.

Since I was the oldest out of five, I eventually became responsible for looking out for my siblings. That responsibility took on the form of making sure I gave them their drinks and snacks before I could eat on road trips, to babysitting them while my Mother was at work. This meant sacrificing doing what young girls liked and needed to do. Instead of reading a book, I would be washing clothes and cleaning the house. When my friends were hanging out and having fun, I stayed home and looked out for my brothers and sister. At the time, I did not see anything wrong with it, because it was what my Mother needed me to do; however, I later realized that my childhood memories went from riding bikes and playing in the park, to carrying adult responsibilities on my shoulder. Sounds like a rough and unfair childhood, but really my life experience after my

Father died taught me how to persevere and show more empathy to others.

Life is not always fair, but if you have made it through just one challenging situation, then you can get through them all. You see if you realize that you are like a diamond where each painful experience converges to enlighten your life and build your mental strength; half the battle is won. I have learned over the years that life will bury you deep within the Earth's crust under conditions of intense heat and pressure and you have to decide if you are going to labor and toil through each challenge in order to crystallize and combine each into the gem that you were created to be. You are an incredibly rare, unbreakable, pure and uniquely valuable individual – a diamond. Life is tough but each mountain you choose to overcome reinforces your mental strength and understanding. No matter how many challenges you face your ability to persevere and conquer is strengthened, if you remember how successful you were at overcoming previous challenges.

When I started this single parent journey almost thirteen years ago, trusting that God would provide the wisdom and strength I needed to raise my children, my past experiences reminded me that I could do this. I had no idea how, but I knew I could do it. If nothing more, I understood the sacrifice necessary to raise confident, intelligent, strong, responsible and loving children.

Needless to say, this was a very challenging time for me, and I was extremely sad due to what my children were going through. I remember the feeling of growing up without my Father and I did not want my children to go through the same misery. In the beginning, it seemed like the boys would have the best of both worlds, but eventually that turned out to be nothing more than a dream. It was, and still is my worst nightmare. I had hoped that despite the separation, that we both could be there just like we were before, to some degree, but the boys were with me most of the time. I was so sad, and my heart literally cried for them. I understood all too well, that no child should have to grow up without consistent interaction with their parents. I had to deal with it because my Father died, but for the life of me, I did not want the kids to grow up without either me or my ex-husband. So, even though the boys' father was not there as much as I thought he should be, I made it a point to let them go with him whenever he could pick them up – even if it meant canceling Christmas or vacation plans.

I must credit this to my Grandpa. My Grandpa had intentionally and carefully taught me to love but put boundaries in place. In doing so, he placed a wall of protection around me. I did not know it and could not see it until I started going through my divorce, but my Grandfather was preparing me for a world that was cruel and would attempt from every angle to distract me from my destiny. You see if I had taken the position to be angry about my ex-husband's inconsistency in spending time with the boys, then I would have totally disregarded what my children needed – both parents. I swallowed my pride and realized that the same sacrifice that I made when I was younger was going to have to be kicked up a level. I had to learn not to judge my ex-husband and swallow my pain at the same time so that I would not interfere with whatever type of relationship their Father had chosen to build with them. It was not ideal because I felt like he (their father) needed to be there more, but it was also his choice. I remember the day their father came by the house with his car packed to say goodbye to the boys. He was leaving Virginia and moving to California. This was the boys first time hearing of this and I just could not believe that he would tell them like this, nor could I believe he was actually going to move to the other side of the country and be even further away from them. So, this meant they were going to go from seeing him sporadically to not at all. I was not ready to see them go through this and I threw a fit. I have no idea what I said to him, because all I could see was red. They were fifteen and eleven, having to deal with another level of not having their father around. I was furious but realized all I could do was focus on what I needed and could do, for them.

I decided to give 100% of myself to raising and providing for them. I understood that the ultimate sacrifice was going to involve forgiving their father yet again for not being there for the boys as I thought he should be. Forgiveness and ignoring the distraction was imperative so that I could focus on making sure they had the best possible life. I did not have the slightest clue why my Grandpa would constantly preach "to forgive people". He would say, "This world is full of people and things that will constantly throw negativity and hate towards you, but you have to forgive them and love anyway because if you do not, you will block your blessings." I really did not understand this concept until I had to put it into practice. I now know the power of forgiveness. No matter what anyone says or does - forgive so you can free yourself to focus on what you need to focus on.

Forgiveness was my ultimate sacrifice, but it was by no means the only sacrifice. For seven years, I worked four jobs:

- 1st job - my kids
- 2nd job – my main job
- 3rd job – overtime at my main job
- 4th job – security gig

My friends called me the "Jamaican woman", because I was always working multiple gigs on top of doing what I had to do as a parent. There were some days I did not get any sleep, because I was serious about making sure I attended every teacher conference, participated in the PTA, attended every football or soccer practice, went to football and soccer games, attended track meets, drove across town every Sunday to take one to Chinese lessons, traveling to New York for modeling competitions, attended every orchestra concert, worked the concession stands, taught them how to drive, took them to tutoring sessions, walked the floor at night when they were sick – yes, the full sacrifice. And I enjoyed every single second of it! Being a Mom was my primary job and I wanted to make sure I put everything I had into creating a better life for myself and my children.

I was in my early thirty's and I was left to fend not only for myself but for two young black boys in Northern Virginia – the fastest moving area besides New York and LA. Yes, all by myself. Needless-to-say, life was challenging. I mean I did not have a clue on where to begin and only a few family and friends to support me. Realizing that I had to find a balance to be everything for my children was overwhelming. So many questions and doubts:

- How do I discipline them and let them know that the discipline was necessary, out of love?
- How do I help them with their homework and work multiple jobs?
- How do I forgive their Father and show them to love in-spite of?
- How do I teach the boys to not let adversity win?
- How do I teach these boys to be courageous despite their situation?
- How do I protect them from folks' obvious and the subtle attacks aimed at tearing down their dreams and aspirations?
- How do I teach them to always hope and keep the faith?
- How do I teach them to be respectful and except nothing less than the respect you deserve?
- How do I teach them to "man up" and have integrity?
- How do I?

I finally stopped and asked God for help. One night as the tears were rolling down the side of my face and onto my pillow, I decided that it was really time to depend on God to help me with raising these two great gifts. I prayed and fasted while asking for guidance and wisdom on how the three of us could positively move on with our lives.

One day, shortly after praying this prayer, I was at my Grandma Bess' birthday party. I went to say hi to her and as I kneeled down to hug her, she said, "Tanita (lol, that is what she used to call me) how you doing, baby?" And before I could answer she said, "Let me tell you something. You focus on taking care of you and your two boys. I know that it is not easy, and it all seems unfair, but you cannot make anyone be there for you, but you must be there for yourself and your boys. I mean really be there." I said, "yes, ma'am." She said, "Don't pay any attention to what folks are doing or not doing for you. You have everything within you to make a good life for you and your boys". She went on to say, "Everything happens for a reason, baby, but at some point, you have to start living your best life." I drove back to Virginia thinking about this and decided on the drive back home that this dark moment of feeling victimized had to go. My Grandmother's discernment saved my life and opened the possibility for me to fight for the sake of my life and children's life. We moved beyond the realm of simply being survivors to being fortunate in that all three of us are more confident, extremely grateful, and unstoppable concerning the challenges and drama that come with life.

Here is another useful activity that is helpful in strategizing on how to move forward.

INSTRUCTIONS: Use this worksheet to brainstorm new ideas to move you closer to a goal or habit change. Do your best to come up with the full five actions or behaviors – one for each box below – completing the worksheet, in any order. Remember this is brainstorming, so just because you write it down does not mean you have to do it – we are just looking for potential ideas to move you forward! To wrap up this exercise, circle the actions you like the look of – or WILL do!

Date: _____

What is your goal, why are you brainstorming actions?

I want to

_____

Thinking about your goal, what could you:

	STOP doing	Do Less of	Keep doing	Do More of	Start Doing
1					
2					
3					
4					
5					

Unwavering Faith

Selah: And he said unto me, My grace is sufficient for thee: for my strength is made perfect in weakness.

While teaching my children how critical tenacity is to achieving success in every area of their life, I quickly realized being a single Mom had its rewards and stigmatism with the latter having the most impact on our family as a whole. More often than with single Fathers, society looks at single Moms in the following negative ways:

1. **"Single Moms put themselves in this vulnerable position."** No! "Please note that more than half of the single mothers in the U.S. are widowed, divorced, or separated.
2. **"Single Moms only raise kids who turn out to be criminals".** Not exactly! "Some of the most prominent figures in history have single mothers to thank for their upbringing — including former president, Barack Obama".
3. **"Single Moms have low self-esteem and no standards."** Clearly it takes two people to produce a baby?
4. **"Single Moms are broke and on welfare."** Not all of them. "Single motherhood has grown so common in America that today 80 percent of single-parent families are headed by single mothers — nearly a third of those, live in poverty." Where does that leave the other 66 percent?

(https://singlemotherguide.com/single-mother-statistics/)

5. **"Single Moms are of no value and will never amount to anything."** It is this type of judgmental behavior that sometimes discourages single Moms. They already have enough on their plate and instead of twisting one's thumb on someone who is already facing a challenging task, you would think those around the single Mom would seek ways to edify and show some empathy. Despite this type of negativity, Moms who understand they are not victims but have the power within themselves to empower themselves and their children can and will accomplish anything. Yes, they will have to face the fact that society expects for them to operate as a two-parent household. It is amazing that people understand that a car needs both chargers plugged up to a car battery for a car to run properly, but totally ignores that a single mom needs support. She has to work at ensuring her family has the finances to maintain some normalcy, go to every soccer practice, rush to Sunday afternoon Chinese language practice, teach her children to love themselves so that bullies(adults and other children alike) do not kill their dreams/destiny, protect them from predators, take time to exercise, hang out with friends.

6. **"Single Moms" Well, this time I must modify...., "Single Beautiful Christian Moms",** who simply want to give their children a church family to hopefully feel a part of, endure the jealousy and judgement of almost everyone in the church. They are looked down on and treated as loose jezebel women

from the time they step in the church until they find settle in their car after the service.

At some point, I have experienced all the above, but I used each hurtful moment to empower myself and therefore my children. In the beginning, I felt so hopeless and then I realized this tough situation was not going to define who I was or who I was going to become. The poison did not kill me, it made me more immune. Even more importantly, it would not define my two young men's destiny. A challenge on so many different levels, because at the beginning stages of the divorce I realized this pain we were all enduring was not about me but more about breaking generational curses. My family and my ex-husband's family had a plethora of situations and sins which distracted family members from operating in their greatness. I am thankful I realized the divorce and the treatment we received following the divorce happen so my children and I could understand our purpose. I was determined to defy the odds by discovering and operating in my greatness. My decision to seek greatness and ignore the negativity no matter what changed the trajectory of my life and my two sons.

Overcoming Mindset

Selah - See then that ye walk circumspectly, not as fools, but as wise, Redeeming the time, because the days are evil. Ephesians 5:15-16

Often, single parents do not have the support system they need and even more debilitating, society does not stop to consider the pressures that single parents go through. It really is a sink or swim situation. Now, each single parent household requires a different type of support. Some may require financial support, family engagement or emotional support. Whatever the need it is usually not available from those around them. There are all kinds of reasons for a support system not being in place (i.e., people are too busy with their own lives and family, people simple do not understand what they are not experiencing, people see single parents with equal capabilities as two-parent households). When I started my divorce, I prayed and asked God to send Godly men who would impart wisdom, confidence and love into my two young men. The hands on, dig deep work I knew I had to do. However, I understood that even with all the work I would put into raising my sons, it may not actually be enough. Why? Because they were boys that needed to become strong confident men.

- Men who were reliable and dependable and understood what it meant to take the lead and do what is right or regardless of what challenges they faced.
- Men who understood that if they chose to place God first and foremost in their hearts that nothing would be impossible.

- Men who understood in a harsh world they could still be winners despite the challenges and difficulties they would face.
- Men who loved themselves and would take time to understand themselves and know without a shadow of doubt God's love for them.

During my youngest son's senior year, my job moved me to Colorado. Instead of leaving KD in Virginia I uprooted him from what he knew as home, his friends, his school and football team of his entire high school years. I could have let him stay in Virginia and avoided all this, but I did not want to leave him behind. We arrived in Colorado and KD got off to a good start with school, sports and meeting new friends. He actually played football and soccer at the same time while adjusting to a different time zone and elevation. A few days before football playoffs, KD's entire football career hit its culmination. My son had played football since he was four years old and faced a lot of opposition due to his size and the fact that I was a single mother. Through the tears, mistreatment and frustration he managed to stay focused and to excel in the sport. One evening his football season conflict with four offensive linemen highlighted his entire football struggle.

All season I had been giving him advice on how to deal with these bullies. During one practice, a couple of 300-pound lineman teammates decided they were going to take KD's helmet and put it in the middle of the field. KD saw the lineman as he was taking it to the middle of the field and started screaming for him to put the helmet back. Although the coaches heard the altercation they did not intervene and the two (my 170 lb. son and the 300 lb. lineman) entered a stalemate. The lineman left the helmet on the field and KD refused to go move it. When the entire team started to run suicide drills the head coach asked, "whose helmet is this?" KD replied, "It's mine, but you need to make the lineman move it back where he got it from." The coach proceeded to let my son know if he did not pick up the helmet before he (the coach) reached it he (the coach) was going to kick KD off the field. KD did not move and was surprised that the coach was only addressing him instead of everyone involved. The coach reached the helmet before KD, picked the helmet up, threw it across the field and said, "F*** you KD and your f*****-up principles." My son took off his pads, threw them on the field and left.

When I arrived home, I was surprised to hear KD coming downstairs. I asked him why he was not at football practice. The first thing he said to me was "I am going to need you to go to that school and act like you are a country lady from North Carolina." I knew whatever happened at football practice must have been horrifying because both of my sons absolutely hate to see me act like some psycho country lady who only sees red. I braced myself for the absolute worst. He replayed the entire situation to me. I was furious at how the coach handled this and wanted to go to the football field right then and there. Although I was furious, I wanted to make this a teaching moment. At this point, I also asked my son if there was anything different he could have done to avoid this situation going south so quickly. KD looked at me and said, "I am tired, Mom." He went on to say that he had tried all year to first figure out why the linemen did not like him and then decided to just accept it but refused to accept the disrespect from the coach or the linemen. My son said, "The way they treated me hurt at first but I realized I had not done anything to them. Usually I just ignored them, but this, I was not going to ignore". I sighed and said, "Okay". I told my son at that moment I was proud of him for being strong and I understood why he stood up for himself and spoke against what he had been taught to believe about himself. I always taught the boys not to let anyone treat them less than who they are, and they had every right to stand up to anyone or anything they thought was in opposition to this.

Of course, I scheduled a meeting right away with the coach and Assistant Principal. The coach denied throwing the helmet and cursing at my son. To add insult to injury, the coach went on to say all season he wanted to meet with me because he felt like my son's home life was impacting his football performance. Already fuming over this coach lying about what happened on the football field the previous evening, I asked, "How so?" He went on to say, "I figured that since your son comes from a single parent household that he may be facing some challenges that the other football players do not face." Of all the things that were discussed my son knew I was going to blow a gasket when the coach made a comment about our single parent condition. My son sat back, laughed and said, "Man you have messed up now." I smiled and said, "Do share!" The coach replied, "Well, for example, earlier in the season (not the whole season but earlier), KD would fall asleep and I figured that this was due to KD either having to work in the evening to help with bills or because he went the bed whatever time he wanted to because you, the single Mother, may be working two jobs." I laughed and immediately went into my red zone. I explained to the coach that his prejudice towards myself and my son was inappropriate and was going to stop as we were speaking. I explained to him that my child would not be mistreated because of your ignorance. I informed him that we lived in a four bedroom house located in a golf community only five minutes from the school and that my son had a homemade dinner waiting for him each night when he came home from football. I advised the coach how ridiculous his assumptions were and how disappointed I was in him as a black coach who should be looking for any opportunity to uplift young black males. I told him that my son was one of two black males on the team and instead of making my son feel like he did not belong, he could have at least respected my son as a human being. I went on to say, "And to put the cherry on top, you have the audacity to sit in this meeting and attempt to paint a picture that something is wrong with my son because his mother is single, while I sit here in your face." The anger and contempt I felt at this time towards the coach was also a culmination of feelings I had overcome my entire journey as a single mother.

The coach attempted to defend himself and stated he did not mean to imply that coming from a single parent household was a bad thing. I stressed to him it did not matter what he intended but it had everything to do with what I was hearing and perceiving at this very moment. I asked the Assistant Principal if any other teacher or coach at the school had complained about my son's behavior because he was from a single-family home. The Assistant Principal said "No" and remarked that everyone loved my son and spoke how polite and well-mannered he was. I looked over at the coach and I said to him as I was pointing at my son, "I don't know what kind of show you are putting on for these linemen and their parents but you and them will stop bullying my son today!" The coach was still caught up in his fantasy and said, "I cannot control the other players." At which point I advised if it was not taken care of, I would do it myself even if it meant calling the local news to make this public.

As I was walking to my car the coach ran out to apologize to me for his insulting comments concerning my current state as a single Mom. Just as I open my mouth to respond to the coach my son was standing beside me and advised the coach that if he laid a hand on his Mom he would no longer be talking. I explained to my son I was okay, but my son refused to go back to class until he saw me get in my car. Later that day, the secretary called to let me know that she had seen the entire exchange and wanted me to know I had raised a phenomenal young man. My son no longer had any issues from that moment on and we became the talk of the town. I had other coaches calling to apologize for this type of behavior and advised that they stood behind me and applauded my position. Parents of my son's teammate would stop me in the grocery store and comment on their son's admiration for KD and his bravery to stand up to the coach and these linemen.

What would happened if I did not have the mindset to question the coach's actions and the understanding to be an advocate for my children? I credit a lot of my mental strength to my ancestors. They truly laid the foundation for me to build a positive, faithful outlook on life. In that one meeting and in a manner of seconds everything that my Grandfather, Grandmothers, Father and Mother taught me about myself rose up within me. I could hear my Grandfather saying, "You can do anything you put your mind to do and you can do it better than anyone else." I could hear my Grandmother Cotten saying, "You are always so strong and always speak your mind, but in love." I could hear my Grandma Bess saying, "Everything happens for a reason baby, but at some point, you have to start living your best life." And as far as I was concerned, my children and I were living a great life considering the hand we were dealt and I was not about to let some coach sit here and taint all the hard work I had put into raising my sons and providing for them. I could hear my Father saying, "You are my princess and there is only one of you." This is what kept me smiling during my entire rant. I could hear my Mother saying, "No one is better than you," and my voice reminded me to let it be known.

My son kept pushing and despite the opposition he was named the defensive player of the year in the state of Colorado and earned a scholarship to play football in college. At the same time, we found out about my son's scholarship, we saw on the news that this same coach was arrested for stealing over a million dollars. Out of curiosity, I asked my son how he felt about the coach getting arrested. My son said, "I feel sorry for him and mostly for his son who is actually a nice kid." I quietly did a sigh of relief, smiled and told my son how proud I was of him for not holding a grudge against the coach.

We both faced a distraction that could have derailed KD's opportunity to accomplish his dreams altogether. When you are working toward a goal or dream, negative things will attempt to impede your progress. This is not the time to give up or attempt to get revenge. In fact, it is time to press forward even harder, because the greatest battles always come when you are closest to achieving your goals. Do not let the distractions win by giving up but instead keep working towards making your dreams come true.

When you have unwavering faith and determination, it cultivates a mindset that makes you unstoppable no matter what is happening. A mindset that embodies high self-esteem, love, confidence, courage and perseverance. Here is how I did it:

1. I wrote down who I was, minus all the chaos, by reminding myself what my ancestors taught. I made a commitment to start living life to the fullest. I deserved this.

2. I started journaling each night. This help me deal with my emotions. I was able to clearly see the difference between the facts and the emotions.

3. I posted positive affirmations about myself on the bathroom mirror. Having the affirmations in the bathroom was a constant reminder for me to keep speaking positively. This empowered me to make decisions that have led to my success.

4. I started working out to make sure I was physically capable of taking care of myself, my children and everything that came with being a single Mom. I know this one may seem like an odd ball but going for a run in the neighborhood or simply taking time to lift weights was empowering and made me feel like I could accomplish anything.

5. I started sharing with my friends how I was feeling and was relieved to hear what I was going through was nothing new under the sun. I leaned on my friends and allowed their love to validate who I was. Sometimes hearing it from those who love you is the right kind of medicine to help you rediscover your confidence and love of yourself.

I took a leap of faith to work on myself. This propelled me to understand everything I needed was already inside of me. I just needed to put it to work. To my surprise when I felt better about myself more opportunities came my way.

A friend of mine reached out one day and asked if I had thought about applying for a job that offered a higher income. I explained it was appealing but my teaching position allowed me to spend more time with my children. She then mentioned I could request a flexible schedule. I really needed to make more money, so I applied for the job which was completely outside of my current teaching career. Within months I excepted the position and making three times my current salary. I was so excited and could now provide a better life for myself and my children.

And, so, the journey presented itself thirteen years ago and I was horrified. For years, I had always been taken care of by a higher being and I had to remind myself that the same God who took care of me when I lost my father at eight years old, when my entire family, with the exception of my Grandfather who died in 2008, turned their back on me after I decided to get married, when family decided to ridicule me and not be there when I had my first son, when false rumors were spread about why I got a divorce, when I had to protect my sons from every demonic spirit and human being who saw them as vulnerable or when the high school football coach said that he usually only let recruiters know about football players whose parents are still together. So, where did all the adversity leave my children who are from a single mother household? My children who could clearly see the disadvantage of coming from a single mother household, but decided they were still going to put forth their best effort, have a great attitude and above all remain faithful to the process. The latter sums it up. My sons, like any children, wanted the best… car, house, money, start on football team and clothes…you name it. It was painful seeing others with the bigger house, more exotic vehicles, fancier clothes, two parents in the house – only because my boys did not always have the exact same. We were not poor, but we did not have the million-dollar house either. However, it was exhilarating to know that we had each other and that meant more than all the fancy cars and houses.

The Greatest Investment

Selah: I AM ...the First & the Last. Depend and trust in me and watch the miracles happen. Humble yourself and understand that I have given you, my daughter, a spirit of power and of love and of a sound mind.

The greatest investment anyone can make is to invest in themselves. To say that this is challenging for single parents is quite an understatement. Single parents are solely responsible for providing everything that their children. Most single parents work extra hours to provide the basic needs like food and shelter. There is the constant struggle to balance parenting responsibilities with having a career, creating enough income, feeling guilty, prioritizing time and developing emotional stability. All of these are important and must be fulfilled. Depending on the parent and the children, the balancing act will vary. Here are some ways I managed to balance my responsibilities:

> **1. Emotional Stability - Realize the King/Queen in You:** Developing emotional stability, in my opinion, is by far the foundation to the balancing act. As a single parent the realization that no one will match your expectation for the care of yourself and your children is quicky realized. No one really understands how overwhelming it can be to take on this type of responsibility by yourself. You love your children and want to see them do well. You give them a fighting chance by keeping your emotions in check. When I got over myself, I realized the divorce was not who I was and definitely not who I was becoming.

The moment I came to terms with this I had more clarity and awareness of what my children were experiencing.

2. Creating Enough Income - Sole Bread Winner: Going from a two-income household to one income is difficult, especially when you do not have anyone to support you. I really struggled in this area and in hindsight there was one decision that could have given me a better foundation. You know those decisions where you can look back and say, "If I had done this differently, then things would have been better." I discourage the "what ifs" because there is nothing you can do about what already happened and this journey really helped me to understand that everything has a purpose and is necessary.

However, the boys and I would have done much better financially and emotionally if I stayed in our home instead of selling it. I was advised by a divorce lawyer to sell the home because it would alleviate having something in my ex-husband and my name and it would make the divorce proceedings less cumbersome. I was working as a teacher and did not have enough money to cover everything for the family. After school care on one income was not feasible. I wish I had done more research to find every possible option to find childcare but got caught up in the disappointment of not having help with our children – not my children but *our* children. I allowed the disappointment and shock of non-support from my children's father to literally block my ability to find other resources to cover this expense. This is why I stress the importance of not getting distracted.

Meeting this expense would have allowed us to stay in our home and would have kept some normalcy for the boys. There was no stability in the family and home, and I let emotions overcome me as well. I wanted to sell our home because I did not think I could afford it without the support of my ex, and I totally was not thinking about my children. The best thing for them would have been to stay in our home.

Due to this one decision, my children and I moved a lot over the next four years. I was fortunate that they were well-mannered children and I basically did not have a lot of behavior issues as a result of the constant moving. I was not able to get us back in a home until 2010. I lost a lot of money from moving around a lot, but the boys and I became closer due to our mutual desire to overcome and get back to having our own home instead of renting a friend's basement or an apartment. One pet-peeve I developed from this experience was to never let your emotions drive your decision on staying in your home. It is the one safe-haven and consistency your children need.

At one point, while renting a friend's basement to hopefully save money to buy our next home, I found a note that my oldest son had written to God. It said, "God, please bless us with a home. We don't even have a window to look out of and my Mom does not have her own bed." I was devastated. Here I was thinking that the boys would be okay staying in this big house, but they were not happy. To make matters worse my friend's Mom came to stay and started telling my friend that I was looking down on her (my friend). Here I was living in the basement but looking down on someone? With these two realities glaring down my throat, I immediately started looking for our own place and we moved to a condo close to my job. But we had to stay with some other friends for a few weeks until the place became available.

Although we were only supposed to be at the friends for a few weeks, one morning before I dropped the boys off to school, I found a letter on top of their lunch boxes. It said, "I saw that you bought the boys expensive cinnamon buns from the Cinnabon store in the mall. If you have money to take them to the mall and treat them then you could at least give us a little something for staying here. You are not the only one that wants cinnamon buns." I was in complete shock. The tears started rolling right away, because I was not trying to get over on anyone and I was surprised that these people who had opened their home up to us for a few weeks would leave me a letter instead of talking to me face to face. I tucked the letter in my purse and decided I would talk to them about it when I got home that evening. After I got the boys settled in for bed that night I spoke to the wife and she advised me that she had written the letter. I explained to her that I was willing to pay for the time that we were at their place and that I really appreciated them helping me out until the new place was available. I went on to say that the Cinnabon treats were a reward to the boys for holding up their end of the deal in getting their schoolwork done and being so well-mannered during this transition. It had nothing to do with whether I could afford it or not, but everything to do with me letting my children know I was so proud of their strength and maturity despite the situation. She apologized and explained how challenging this must be for them and me right now. If you get nothing else out of this story, please believe me when I say if you have your own home, fight to stay in it for the sake of your children. Do not let anyone convince you otherwise. The pain still resonates today, but I realize it was an ill-informed mistake on my part. My intentions were sincere and that is what helped me to push past that mistake and stay focused on what I was working to achieve. The goal was to establish a good life for my children and I, despite the lack of support.

The condo we moved into was more expensive, but at least the boys had their own room and I was close to their schools during the workday, in case I needed to get to them quickly.

Not long after moving closer to my job, my supervisor advised that there was a need for travel out of the area and so I faced the childcare issue again. Reluctantly, I reached out to their father to see if he would watch them at my place to avoid uprooting them again. The response was again, shocking. "No, I will not help you with that." It was almost as if I was asking a stranger to watch his own children. My cousin who was truly a blessing to the boys and I, wanted to hear this shocking news for herself too. When I arrived in North Carolina she asked me to call him so she could ask him herself to watch them while I was traveling. I called and put him on speaker. When he responded with exactly what I had told her and her Mom (my Auntie), she asked him, "Why?" and he replied, "Because that is something she must figure out." My cousin looked at me in awe and said, "Hang up the phone! I cannot believe he will not watch his own children while you are traveling!" The boys lived with family in North Carolina for about four months while I was traveling. I came to North Carolina every weekend if I was not traveling for business, but this was the hardest and most heartbreaking experience ever. We needed the income, so I did what I had to do. When the travel stopped, we returned to Virginia.

Currently I am numb with excitement and achievement. It is all so surreal. My prayers were answered, and God provided me the wisdom and courage to show my two young men the importance of surviving their parents' divorce and the need for perseverance. In 2019, I witnessed my oldest graduate from college with a Bachelor of Science degree in Radiology. My youngest graduate from high school as Defensive Football Player of the Year with a scholarship to play football in college. He decided to join the Marine Corp and has completed his training. To my surprise, many congratulated me on a job well done, but let me tell you that although I was a proud Mama, these guys were the ones who put in the hard work. I owe my children success all to God and to my sons who continued to stay positive, hopeful and fight for what they wanted despite the challenges. Yes, I had a lot to do with their success, but it was due to the wisdom God gave me as a single Mom.

3. Avoiding Guilt – Stop with the What Ifs: One thing that is very true is that you cannot change the past. Why waste valuable time focusing on what you cannot change. As a single parent the three main areas I felt guilty about for a long time were:

a. Not ensuring that my children had two parents in the household. This literally kept me up many nights contemplating what to do in the early stages of the separation. My sons were great kids and deserved to have both parents in the home. However, in between the time when the boys' father and I were finally separated to the divorce, I realized the home was a lot more peaceful. No more fussing or hostility for the children to witness. Instead, we had a safe haven to start healing and getting connected with who we were as individuals and as a family.

b. Letting my emotions get to me and listening to others about selling our home: I wish I had done more research on how to find ways to meet all the family obligation to keep the home for the sake of the boys.

c. Working so much: I literally worked four jobs at one point. I have no idea how, but I did. I wanted to make sure I could provide a decent life for my children. This meant I was away from them more than I wanted to be. I felt so horrible. Then one day I had to remind myself that at least I had a job. I also was able to put the boys into the extracurricular activities that they were interested in, keep food on the table, send them on mission trips, go on vacations and the like.

4. Prioritizing Time – Scheduling the Time:

Although I had to work a lot, it was imperative that I spent time with the boys. I developed a rather strict schedule to include what time the boys had to be in the bed, to movie time on Friday night. The schedule was imperative to spend time with them and to make sure I showed up. I did not care what was going on I made sure I showed up to football games to the principal office with the same type of mentality. Giving up what was comfortable for me so that my children could live the best life possible. There is something that changes when you become a parent. It did not matter if it was peaches and cream to deal with or drama happening all around, I decided to sacrifice, love, pray and be there for my children no matter what.

5. Managing Your Career – I was fortunate to transition from my teaching career to a career that had better benefits, better salary and a plethora of opportunities to make additional funds. This was so powerful all within itself and God was really looking out for me. The fact that I earned my Master's in Technology Management versus just having a high school degree, made it possible for us to live a decent life.

Totally not the life I had envisioned, but I am extremely grateful for how well life turned out for all three us. I honestly can say that my decision to remain positive, focus on what my children needed and desired, actively look for ways to make the impossible happen and preserver regardless of the roadblocks and lack of support shaped a better life for us.

Mind Battles: The Law of Attraction

Selah: For we *wrestle not against flesh and blood, but against principalities, against powers, against the rulers of the darkness of this world, against spiritual wickedness...understand who you are really battling with and watch what you think, say and do. Ephesians 6:12*

Have you ever said, "I don't ever see myself getting out of this." Or, "Why is this happening to me?" Or, "No one cares." Or, "Why is everyone else successful and I am not." Or, maybe you are anxious and afraid of what may or may not happen.

This type of thinking is what I call the *abyss energy*. It is what hurts and disturbs our inner peace and leads us to a dark place that serves no purpose in life or the exact opposite of what we were placed on this earth to do. The mind is a battle ground and we must do everything possible to prepare for this unrelenting battle. Please understand the process of how things happen in our lives. Usually what you think you will eventually speak and it has a chance of coming to fruition.

We take our focus off what we can control and put our valuable energy on external scenarios that we have no control over. STOP!!! That is why it is so important to have clarity on what you are expecting and to maintain consistency until your dreams are fulfilled. You have to focus on the positive and push forward no matter what is happening around or to you. This is hard to do and you will feel frustrated, sad and alone at times. If you stay focus on the positive and trust that it will all work out for your good, you will eventually see the manifestation. At some point you must realize what you envision in your mind will likely become your reality. What does this really look like? Well, when I first divorced, I was overwhelmed with sadness and afraid that I would not have what it took to take care of my two boys. I had to convince myself I could make life rewarding for all three of us, but it was going to require conscious effort for us to live a happy abundant life. I did not know how our life was going to be, but I was determined to make it the best I could. Yes, I made up in my mind that I was going to will happiness into our life, and it worked. It worked! Now, let me tell you we went through a series of unfortunate events but each time we came out on top with lessons we could directly and indirectly use and teach to others.

Life will throw all kinds of curve balls your way. There will be something you always deal with, but it is important to remember that you are not what happens to you. So often we get caught up in what has happened to us in our past or what is currently happening to us that we unknowingly block where we should be going. When you focus on negativity, scattered, self-sabotaging, judgmental, addictive and energy draining things you stagnate your growth. It is time to leave your past behind. Let everything go that is hindering you from moving forward. You must have the mindset that you will have a great life because you deserve it and be intentional in living your best life no matter what. This takes practice and is not an overnight process, but it is necessary to build your faith and confidence in who you are. In the next chapter, I will discuss the importance of understanding who you are. I want to share some activities you can practice in developing the positive mindset you need to overcome anything that seeks to destroy your very existence. Let me be clear. The thoughts you allow to linger and the language you use every day represents and impacts how you experience your world. To capture thoughts, ideas, and describe what you see around you inevitably gets lost in translation. Information through generalizations, omission of details, and cognitive distortion is all done consciously and unconsciously. How we choose to manage information provides underlying beliefs about ourselves, others and the world we live in. Take a look at the top 10 cognitive distortions and be honest with yourself. **Check the areas below that you might need to change or improve.**

Top 10 Cognitive Distortions

1. **All or Nothing Thinking:** Seeing things as black-or-white, right-or-wrong with nothing in-between. Essentially, if I'm not perfect then I'm a failure.
    - I didn't finish writing that paper, so it was a *complete* waste of time.
    - There's no point in playing *if I'm not 100%* in shape.
    - They didn't show up, they're *completely* unreliable!

2. **Overgeneralization:** Using words like always, never in relation to a single event or experience.
    - I'll *never* get that promotion
    - She *always* does that...

3. **Minimizing or Magnifying (Also Catastrophizing):** Seeing things as dramatically more or less important than they are. Often creating a "catastrophe" that follows.
    - *Because* my boss publicly thanked her, she'll get that promotion, not me (even though I had a great performance review and just won an industry award).
    - I forgot that email! *That means* my boss won't trust me again, I won't get that raise and my wife will leave me.

4. **"Shoulds":** Using "should", "need to", "must", "ought to" to motivate oneself, then feeling guilty when you don't follow through (or anger and resentment when someone else doesn't follow through).
   - I *should have* gotten the painting done this weekend.
   - *They ought to* have been more considerate of my feelings, *they should know* that would upset me.

5. **Labeling:** Attaching a negative label to yourself or others following a single event.
   - I didn't stand up to my co-worker, *I'm such a wimp!*
   - *What an idiot*, he couldn't even see that coming!

6. **Jumping to Conclusions:**

   1) **Mind-Reading:** Making negative assumptions about how people see you without evidence or factual support.
   Your friend is preoccupied, and you don't bother to find out why. You're thinking:
   - She *thinks I'm exaggerating* again, or
   - He still *hasn't forgiven me* for telling Fred about his illness.

   2) **Fortune Telling:** Making negative predictions about the future without evidence or factual support.
   - I *won't be able* to sell my house and *I'll be stuck* here (even though housing market is good).
   - *No-one will understand. I won't be invited back* again (even though they are supportive friends).

7. **Discounting the Positive:** Not acknowledging the positive. Saying anyone could have done it or insisting that your positive actions, qualities or achievements don't count...
   - That *doesn't count, anyone* could have done it.
   - I've *only* cut back from smoking 40 cigarettes a day to 10. *It doesn't count* because I've not fully given up yet.

8. **Blame & Personalization:** Blaming yourself when you weren't entirely responsible or

blaming other people and denying your role in the situation
- *If only I was* younger, I would have gotten the job
- *If only I hadn't* said that, they wouldn't have...
- *If only she hadn't* yelled at me, I wouldn't have been angry and wouldn't have had that car accident.

9. **Emotional Reasoning:** I feel, therefore I am. Assuming that a feeling is true - without digging deeper to see if this is accurate.
   - I feel such an idiot (it must be true).
   - I feel guilty (I must have done something wrong).
   - I feel bad for yelling at my partner, I must be really selfish and inconsiderate.

10. **Mental Filter:** Allowing (dwelling on) one negative detail or fact to spoil our enjoyment, happiness, hope etc
    - You have a great evening and dinner at a restaurant with friends, but your chicken was undercooked and that *spoiled the whole* evening.

I am convinced that your best life starts when you get over yourself and say goodbye to all the toxins (lies, guilt, failures, jealousy, betrayals, people, fear) so you can be free and move forward.

The Law of Energy

Selah: "Finally, brethren, whatsoever things are true, whatsoever things are honest, whatsoever things are just, whatsoever things are pure, whatsoever things are lovely, whatsoever things are of good report; if there be any praise, think on these things." Philippians 4:8

The Law of Energy states that energy is neither created nor destroyed, it is merely transformed from one form to another. Investing in myself was essential because I knew I was the only person the boys had to depend on. I made sure to take every opportunity to work on my character. Improving your character is important when raising children and is the foundation to establishing your family values.

It is very similar to learning how to walk again. I recently broke my foot and completely tore the tendons in my ankle. I had to learn how to walk all over again. Like, literally. But before my Physical Therapist (PT) would allow me to even put pressure on my foot, he wanted me to build and strengthen the muscles in my leg. Since I had not used my leg muscles for a while, every single muscle in that leg had started to develop atrophy. Collectively my glutes, hamstring, calf and achilleas needed strengthening to help my ankle and foot to bounce back as needed. Prior to the injury I ran three to five miles at least three times a week. With no movement from that leg in almost ten months it was impossible to even walk. As much as I wanted to hurry and get back to my running regimen, I had to take baby steps. I believe building our character operates the same way. We should take baby steps daily.

We should be proactive vice reactive in building our character especially in the face of adversity. We should not wait until chaos is present but should be fine tuning our character daily. If you do not prepare, it might take you longer to bounce back from adversity. Just like with my foot and ankle. If I had not taken baby steps with strengthening all the muscles in that leg, then immense complications would have been the outcome.

Just like with our muscles, we must strengthen our character. For example, if you hold grudges, you definitely want to start practicing coping strategies in preparation for when someone does you wrong. You should start practicing how to love others despite what they do or say. I am not saying let people treat you any kind of way but have enough love in heart to understand that everyone is important and deserves to be loved. Everyone makes mistakes, no one is perfect, and everyone has weaknesses. It takes practice to be in this mental space. It takes practice to be and to get into this space. Start with yourself first.

It was important for me to build my character so I could teach my children how to be the best version of themselves by practicing our family values. I invested a lot of alone time, time with counselors, time with friends and with God to instill the following values:

> **1. Courage:** To understand a person's life depends totally on your actions and guidance is daunting and overwhelming. How do you as single mother raise two boys to be productive and reliable citizens in the face of a world who is waiting to say, "I told you they would turn out to be nothing, because they come from a single parent home." I needed courage to face

this challenge head on and even more courage to hide my pain and grief so my children could heal and have a normal childhood. I was not always successful because your kids know when you are not in the best mood. In those moments I made sure to reminded them that both parents loved them, and that our dispute had nothing to do with them. It was important to me that they loved both of us and did not see either of us as the bad parent. I worked hard not to play the victim. I constantly reminded them that we both loved them and encouraged them to pray for both of us.

2. Love: To unconditionally support others through the good and the bad, is love. The mere fact that God created me in His own image and loves me despite all my flaws, gives me no choice but to love myself. The Word says, "So God created man in his own image, in the image of God created He him; male and female created He them" (Genesis 1:27). I would be insane to not love myself. The Almighty…The Alpha and Omega created little old me, and I am going to have the audacity to not appreciate and love myself? I made a pact with myself to start paying just as much attention to myself as I did to my children. I honestly felt like the worst Mom ever when I started focusing on my spiritual, emotional and physical well-being. The more I focused on my needs, the better Mom and role model I became for my children. As my inner strength grew I became a stronger Mom which contributed to my children becoming more well-rounded. Love became easier.

3. **Respect:** A feeling of deep admiration for someone or something elicited by their abilities, qualities, or achievements. It was very important that my two young men were aware how important it was to respect others, but even more important to respect themselves. By showing respect to others, you demonstrated how you expect to be treated. Respect is usually earned and cannot be demanded or forced on anyone.

4. **Integrity:** Is regarded as the honesty and truthfulness or accuracy of one's actions even and especially when no one is looking. It embodies the practice of being honest and showing a consistent and uncompromising adherence to strong moral and ethical principles and values. Principles determine your behavior. For instance, I was passed over for a promotion one year. The reason I did not get the promotion was written on a yellow sticky note and dangled from my personnel folder. The note had two words "personal relationships". I looked up at the HR professional and asked, "What is this and why is it on a sticky note instead of company letter head?" She responded with, "It is on a sticky note because this is not going to be documented in your work record, but the promotion panel wanted to let you know why they did not promote you." I was shocked that this was the reason I was not going to get promoted but reeling with anger that this was the reason why I was being passed over. I worked almost sixty hours a week, my work was completed on time, my clients absolutely loved the timeliness and quality of my work and I got along with just about everyone on my team. I found out from the assistant supervisor that someone had come forward and advised that I was withholding work from

others and as a result none of the clients wanted to work with anyone else This was so far from the truth.

I was hurt and angry someone would paint such a picture of me and that the supervisor would take his word without consulting me. I would have gladly sat down with the man and the supervisor concerning anything involving my moral standards and character. The supervisor said I should have come to them to tell my side of the story. I responded, "I did not even know I had a side of a story to tell." I had to decide at that moment if I was going to continue to be in fifth gear and do my job as I had done before or if I was going to simply skate by and have a negative attitude. I decided to continue getting my work done, but I was very vocal about how unethical this decision was towards me as a person and my career.

From that moment on I focused on actionable measures (i.e., documentation, confronting any negative vibes, metrics tracking) to provide proof on why I should be promoted in the future. The next year I received a bonus and the promotion. I am powerful and great because I live by ethical principles and values that are honest and fair regardless of the situation. I learned it is more beneficial in the long run to abide by your integrity and standards. Under no circumstances should you allow people without integrity to dictate how you live your life. I reinforced the importance of integrity to the boys ever time the opportunity presented itself.

5. Perseverance: Persistence, Tenacity, Determination, Staying Power, Indefatigability, Steadfastness, Purposefulness: I believe the toughest thing for anyone to do is to continue fighting when they are clearly losing, everyone around them is saying they have lost and the situation(s) they are dealing with profoundly unequivocally scream "You are losing and will never bounce back from this." But let me tell you, "You must realize that even when you lose or appear to be losing you must recognize this as an opportunity to dig deep within yourself and find different ways to improve yourself and eventually the situation." I am reminded of my oldest son's desire to earn his degree in Radiology. He studied Radiology since 10th grade in high school. When it came time for him to go to college and finish his degree, he had a moment of doubt. I can remember us having a family meeting one night and with tears in his eyes he said, "Mom I just think I am going to fail." He was the only black male and one of the twelve accepted to the Virginia Commonwealth University (VCU) Radiology program from among over 790 applicants. I was not sure where his fear was coming from. My oldest son always had the most wisdom, courage and confidence of everyone in our family – a Yoda type figure to all of us. I quickly reminded him of all the challenges he had overcome and went over them one by one. By the time we got down to the last few achievements he had already achieved, we were both laughing. I then reminded him of what his Grandpa had always said to us, "You can do this and you…." TK finished it up with "can do it better than anyone else." This gave him the strength to keep pushing.

I am sure there are other values to incorporate in one's life, but these were important values to me. The important thing is to keep working at becoming the best version of yourself. This is going to require baby steps just like I had to take when recovering from my broken foot. It may seem impossible at first, but before you know it you will be stronger and wiser than you ever thought. As I write this, I hear my Grandpa saying, "Baby, make sure you get your education, because once you get that, no one can take it away." Establishing values is very much like getting your education. Once you know what your values are no one can take this from you regardless of what they say or do.

Fail Your Way to Success

*Selah: I can do all things through Christ which strengtheneth me.
Philippians 4:13*

Most people will encounter some type of failure in their life. Life is unpredictable and challenging but should not define you. If you do not remember anything else about this book, please look at yourself and your children as one body. I used to tell my boys that our family is as strong as the weakest link. I needed them to understand that what each one of us did would ultimately impact the entire family. There is no "Mommy spends all her money on purses and red bottoms" and it does not impact TK's technology and science school tuition. Thinking of your family as one unit is as critical as every single vital organ in your body working properly. If fluid builds up in your lungs, then your lungs cannot release oxygen into your blood. In turn, your organs (i.e., heart, lungs, skin) cannot receive enough oxygen enriched blood to function. Every single action – good, bad, indifferent you make will impact the family. We need the best from each other to succeed and thrive. Have the courage to love, to take a chance, to be unique and chase your dreams. Do not allow your ideas to lie dormant. It is time to start living with a sense of urgency. There are no guarantees but what is the benefit of not working towards your dreams? You will either fail or succeed, but if never try you will never know the end results. I challenge you to do all you can physically, mentally and emotionally to succeed in life. Here is how I helped myself and my family get past failure and channel positive energy into our lives:

1. Exploring Activities or New Passions

Do not let any unfortunate life event become who you are but instead discover the new you by exploring new hobbies and activities Make time to do something you have always wanted to do like sky diving, crocheting, weightlifting, painting, or traveling. For instance, I remember saying to a friend how cheerful she was considering her divorce was finalized just last week." I was surprised to hear her respond, "I was sad about the divorce but now I go to dinner almost every weekend for free." She was simply enjoying her new freedom with this fun activity of dating on the weekends.

2. Hear Other People's Opinions but Only Digest What Feeds You.

Other people will judge you and that is okay. Please understand that not everyone will understand your journey nor is it any of their business. It is not their journey to make sense of. It is yours. You cannot change what other people think or say about you. Instead of focusing on changing or correcting other people's opinion of you, surround yourself with positive and supportive people. People who have positive vibes and influence will help you stay positive. Staying positive is so key to succeeding in life. Over the years people have had negative opinions about me but I simply say the opposite and let it go. What people say about you or how they treat you has more to do with issues they are internalizing within themselves than what it has to do with you. I have also learned from experience to quickly cut off negative and no-supportive family and friends.

Remember this is your journey, so why are you letting someone else directly or indirectly influence your life.

3. Perfect Mistakes
No one is perfect and will inevitably make mistakes. In the beginning, middle and until you stop being a parent you will experience a major learning curve. Do your best and understand if you have good intentions you and your children will survive the mistakes. I have had my pity party moments where I absolutely felt like the worst Mom in the world, because I could not give my children all the attention or materialistic things they wanted. I had to step back, breathe and realize that my intentions were in the right place (Selah Moment). I absolutely wanted the best for my children even if it meant I had to do without the necessities (i.e., food & clothes). So, step back and have a Selah moment. You will make mistakes but what parent has not?

4. Establish a Good Relationship with Your Ex
It is necessary to develop a strong co-parenting relationship with the other parent. The children need to see the two people they love the most getting along. This will teach the children how to establish strong relationships with others. Whether you have a good co-parenting relationship with the other parent or not, you must create a safe loving environment for you and your children. You cannot control the other person or force them to see what needs to be done for the children to thrive in life. The only person you can control is yourself. Stay focused on what is ultimately important. If you can, surround yourself

with family and friends who have you and your children's best interest in mind.

5. Keep a Positive Attitude
Be intentional about parenting no matter what is happening. Everything you do should be done with your children's well-being in mind. Demonstrate a positive attitude in front of your children to help build their confidence and self-worth. This is so important to raising healthy and well-rounded citizens.

6. Take Care of Your Children Needs
Since children have less experience with coping skills, you must address their concerns and issues right away. Take them to counseling, find a mentor, hire a tutor or schedule extra time with them.

7. Give Yourself Credit
Reward yourself and work on not be too hard on yourself. Life creates challenges which can be overwhelming It is important to recognize every single win. One win could give you the confidence to overcome other challenges. After you recognize the win then you need to reward yourself. I used to spend $25 a month on jewelry, a pedicure or sushi one Friday night out of the month. Recognizing and rewarding yourself for all your hard work helps you promote kindness and love towards yourself.

We tend to get dragged down and overwhelmed by situations and people. This creates clutter in our minds. You may not want to do anything about what is cluttering your mind but I highly recommend you write them out to raise your awareness on what you need to ignore, fix and resolve.

Make a list of what you are allowing to clutter your mind, drain your energy and slow you down. (i.e., incomplete tasks, frustrations, poor processes and procedures, unresolved issues or problems, other people's or your own behavior, "what ifs", unmet needs, crossed boundaries, poor morale, overdue bills or debt, guilt, poor exercise/eating/sleep habits, office/home cleanliness/tidiness, indecisiveness, procrastination or undone filing). Identify what you are tolerating. Then invest in yourself by stopping others and things from controlling the life you deserve. Make a list and write as many items as you can, then over time as you think of more, simply add them to your list:

WHAT ARE YOU TOLERATING?

1.	2.
3.	4.
5.	6.
7.	8.
9.	10.
11.	12.
13.	14.
15.	16.
17.	18.
19.	20.
21.	22.
23.	24.
25.	26.
27.	28.
29.	30.
31.	32.
33.	34.

The Greatest of These

And now abideth faith, hope, charity, these three; but the greatest of these is charity. 1 Corinthians 12

The foundation to my Being Intentional No Matter What attitude all centers around love. We must learn to forgive and love no matter what. You will likely get mistreated in this life and you must choose the right response to this mistreatment. Your response will determine how abundantly you live your life. If you decide to forgive and love people who mistreat you, then you liberate your mind to focus on your gifts and talents. Your gifts and talents will make room for your dreams to come true. I honestly do not believe I would have been able to achieve so much if I had chosen to hold on to any mistreatment I endured during my life. If you decide to hold grudges and hate people, then you give your power to them and create negative energy which distractions you from focusing on how to use your gifts and talents.

It is very much like the Law of Energy and Law of Attraction discussed in the previous chapter. The energy you put out will be transferred to those around you and/or you will attract the same type of energy, (i.e., the $10,000 check). You really must ask yourself what realm of energy you want to flow in. One of my favorite mini-monologues spells this out very clearly. In the movie, Star Wars, when Yoda talks about young Anakin Skywalker's fear of losing his Mom and Anakin's anger being the reason Yoda did not approve of Anakin becoming a Jedi. In the monologue Yoda says, "Fear leads to anger, anger leads to hate, hate leads to suffering."

Anakin eventually went from being the prophesied Chosen-One, a Jedi with unbelievable powers to serving the dark side as Dark Vader. He killed his wife, lost his kids, and almost dies. How did he get twisted from one extreme to the next? Well, he never let go of his fear of losing his Mother and his anger. This is exactly how life operates. We really must be careful with holding on to feelings like fear and anger and learn to love instead.

I know from first-hand experience how challenging it is to let go of all the spurious deeds done to you and decide to love. It is a choice to not love or to love, but you must choose the latter. I have realized over the years that you can be angry with people for something and they have moved on with their life. You are angry and limiting your life while they are enjoying life.

Another truth which really helps me to understand why I must choose to love is realizing people who hurt other people are hurting people. I have learned to pray for others who do not show me love. This has helped me to love them and move past the hurt. Intellectual Theorist Bell Hooks discusses the struggles people deal with in the following statement. He says, "Anger often hides depression and profound sorrow. Depression often masks the inability to grieve. Males are not given the emotional space to grieve. They are taught to keep it in, and worse, to deny that they feel like crying. Unable to cope with emotional connection, boys internalize the pain and mask it with indifference or rage." This is the reason Anakin gave into the dark side and maybe if he had been given some help with working through his fear and anger, he would have been amongst the best Jedis. We need to be more conscious of these types of realities. I know you may be asking why should you care? My response to this is, have you ever been misunderstood or just needed one person to support or show you compassion?

Love is the answer. It is the message we should exude daily. I am not saying become anyone's doormat. Set your boundaries but be available to love and support. This is true happiness and maturity.

Here are a few activities you can practice daily to love and reclaim your happiness:

1. **Resolve within Yourself** that you are 100% Responsible for what is happening to you.

2. **Build Awareness:** Write down what areas in your life where you are limiting yourself. Once you have identified the areas write three ways you can move past these limits and practice at least one of them for four months. Studies show that if you do something for at least 66 days that it will become a part of you. You will do it without thinking about it.

3. **Develop Long Term Success:** Jot down how long it will take for you to achieve your goals. Will it take you one year or five years? However long you think it will take, on a plain sheet of paper draw a T-shape. On the top left and top right, write 5 years and 10 years respectively. Then underneath both, write your 5-year and ten-year goals.

4. **Surround yourself with good people** who have your best interest in mind. This seems to be the hardest for many people to implement. Mostly because sometimes it can be hard to discern who is for you and who is against you. We are human beings who naturally want to have other human beings in our life, but not everyone

has your best interest in mind. My Grandfather use to say, "In life, you do good, to have two or three good friends."

Your Presence – Their Exposure

Selah - Train up a child in the way he should go and when he is old, he will not depart from it. Proverbs 22:6

After facing so much, I realized I had gained way more than I could have ever imagined. My two sons gave me so much hope and joy. They were the reason I chose to live a happier, stronger, positive and unstoppable life. While they were growing up, I was determined to be my best and live life to the fullest so my children could see what it meant to enjoy and appreciate life. I had committed to being there for my children, but I wanted them to feel my presence even when they could not see or hear me. I intentionally focused on connecting and building a relationship with each one of my children. I wanted them to know no matter what situation they faced; I would always be there for them. The key was getting over myself, realizing what I was going through did not define me and understanding my inner strength. The moment I discovered my greatness was the moment I decided to focus on really being present for my children. I took advantage of every opportunity to connect with my children by listening and asking questions about their day, their friends, their school, their teachers and their extra-curricula activities. My desire was to ensure my children knew they had someone who empathized with what they were going through and someone who wanted the best for them. I was there for them regardless of what they were facing. My voice was just as loud at their football games as it was in the principal office. This is a family value I wanted them to rely on and understand no one could ever take from them. My support was and continues to be unshakeable. Staying connected to them was essential in reassuring them I had their back no matter what and it gave me great insight on how best to push them to their next level.

This insight was essential to my understanding of what opportunities to expose my children to and which external resources would benefit them. It allowed me to set them up for success when they became adults. I purposely sought ways for them to succeed. I wanted them to learn and know for themselves that they had everything inside themselves to succeed and live the life they deserved. Life had thrown all kinds of curve balls our way and despite them hitting me directly in forehead at 100 mph, I was in warrior mode. I realized that through the love and encouragement of my ancestors that I could be who I wanted to be. Not simply because I could work and make it happen, but because I deserved it. This belief was instilled in me at a very young age and I wanted my children to have the same belief embedded in their minds and heart.

While on this journey, I realized sometimes you may have the mental strength to make it happen but lacked the wisdom to handle every single challenge you face. I understood enough to know that I had to get out of my own way to even see how to help myself and my children. So, it was easy for me to let go of all the hurt, fear and pain associated with this unexpected journey, and reach back to what I was always taught both spiritually and naturally. Naturally I understood, "I could do anything I put my mind to if I studied and did my research." The very core of my being believed this due to my Grandpa. Spiritually, I learned over time if I would ask and have faith then God would provide. However, when I realized I would be raising my sons by myself - Like Really

Realized It – my body froze with fear. I quickly realized I had everything within me to overcome whatever came my way. I am so grateful my upbringing and faith in God was so much a part of who I was at thirty-two years old. It allowed me to remain calm and utilize wisdom in raising my two sons and put me in a position to directly and indirectly model how to overcome adversity. This motivated me to work towards excellence and to inspire others to reach their full potential which ultimately prepared me to become a transformational mindset coach.

I constantly sat down and pondered what exposure would benefit the boys. I was not concerned about myself because I knew I would be content as long as they were happy. I made a list of what activities to sign them up for, who they should meet and how to use external resources for their growth, when to emphasize a particular area of interest and where to take them. I purposely decided despite how I was feeling, I was going to take the following actions to ensure they were successful:

1. **Reading the Word of God:** The Word of God is a tool foundational to the power and strength required to live purposefully and I wanted to ensure the boys had an awareness of how to use the Word. Though they may stray away from it, I knew this foundation would be essential to their survival and success as young men. The Word of God protects and covers from the unknowns and knowns, reveals the intent of others and situations, provides guidance on how to deal with any situation, purifies our hearts and provides a template on how we can/should live our best life. I followed a simple process of reading from the bible, encouraging the boys to remember

scriptures and quoting those scriptures to the boys whenever they were going through tough situations.

2. **Pray: "Pray without ceasing"**
    a. (1 Thessalonians 5:17). Pray even when you do not have money. Pray when you do not know where your next meal is coming from. Pray when all your friends leave you. Pray when you have no idea how things are going to turn out. Prayer works and makes a difference in our lives.

3. **Church:** After my divorce, it would have been easy to stay home on Sundays and not deal with the stigmatism church people were dishing out church is supposed to be a safe haven where we all come together to learn God's Word, honor God in worship, and to encourage and be encouraged. Every single church we attended gave my two sons and I the opposite (with the exception of our church in Japan and our church in Northern Virginia). From treating me like I was some jezebel targeting their husbands to assuming my children were boys who had no home training, the church discouraging and unwelcoming. However, I decided that I would push forward for the sake of my children. This was not easy because both of the boys were done with church until we attended Mt. Pleasant Baptist Church in Herndon VA The youth pastor, the magnificent Reverend Brooks, made such an impression on my boys while the senior pastor Rev. James Graham and members poured love on us. We decided to make this our home church. For the first two years, I was known as TK and KD's Mom and was perfectly fine with that. For

those of you still praying and seeking the right church home do not give up. There is a church home for you and your family. My family was tremendously blessed with teachings, edification, and a community of God-fearing people who are still connected with us to this day.

4. **Nourish Their Interest and Gifts:** I have always considered being a Mom, my first job. I spent Sunday through Saturday of every week, over a span of about 20 years, attending parent-teacher conferences, going to Daddy Donuts Day, rushing to Chinese practice, paying for mission medical trips, going to Orchestra concerts, cheering at track meets, going to football practice and games, going to soccer practice and games, teaching them how to drive, pacing back and forth until they arrived home safely from going to the movies with their friends, taking them to college visits, organizing SAT/ACT practice, setting up their dorm and apartments at college. It was a lot to do by myself and at times overwhelming, but I enjoyed every single moment of it. The greatest moments to sum up my joy of being a busy single parent, was going to their room door at night and watching them sleep peacefully. I made sure my kids came first and to expose them to what they were interested in doing.

5. **Spiritual Mentors:** "Iron sharpens iron; so, a man sharpens the countenance of his friend" (Proverbs 27:17). My very first prayer after deciding to be done with the marriage went like this, "Lord please send Godly men into our lives that will and can help the boys grow into young men." My prayers were answered, and the boys had selfless but powerful,

amazing men who all took time to engage and build them up. I am forever grateful for and understand that without these men the boys may not have turned out to be the great people they are today.

Be Intentional No Matter What

Selah - "My grace is sufficient for thee, for my strength is made perfect in weakness. Therefore, I take pleasure in infirmities, in reproaches, in necessities, in persecutions, in distresses for Christ's sake, for when I am weak, then am I strong." 2Corinthians 12:9-11

Life sends many obstacles and challenges & losing the family environment that you are used to is like experiencing the death of a mother or father for a young child. When the boys were eleven and seven years old, I made the hardest decision of my life to completely walk away from my ex-husband. No more praying for it to work, no more believing that this time it will work, no more going to counseling, and no more working on the marriage for the sake of keeping the family together, but definitely time to move forward in order for our lives to escape the emotional roller coaster. An environment that would ultimately hold us all back, including the boy's father, from reaching our full potential.

My heart still aches as I think about the innocence of my sons being washed away with every single tear. As I consoled my sons the tears did not immediately stop but I heard a small voice say, "Constantly read the scripture to your children and around the house." So, I grabbed my bible and through my tears I said to both the boys, "Mommy is so sorry you have to go through this and I want you to know that both your dad and I love you." I went on to explain to them that even though bad stuff happens to us the bad stuff is not who we are, but it is happening to make us stronger. I then read, "My grace is sufficient for thee, for my strength is made perfect in weakness. Therefore, I take pleasure in infirmities, in reproaches, in necessities, in persecutions, in distresses for Christ's sake, for when I am weak, then am I strong. (II Corinthians 12:9-11). Instead of preventing the difficult situation, God used the divorce to strengthen me and the boys. The divorce also helped me realize that all I had to do to help my family (the boys and I) overcome this unfortunate event was to tap into the power that was within me.

It is funny how I always saw my boys as being created for greatness, but it was not until I decided to really be done with attempting to make my marriage work that I saw the greatness in myself. Sometimes we get so caught up in the day-to-day routines of being there for others that we literally become blind to who we are and our purpose here on earth. It is the slow deterioration of one's very soul.

Never let anything or anyone distract you from the great person that you are. When you decide that it does not matter what happens around you or to you, that you are going to believe in yourself and do the work to reach your full potential there is no hurt, shame, lie, jealousy, betrayal that can keep your greatness from coming forth. The legendary actor Cicely Tyson once said, "The moment anyone tries to demean or degrade you in any way, you have to know how great you are. Nobody would bother to beat you down if you were not a threat."

I am reminded of when I first realized this and how others use to say, "She acts like she has never been through anything; like she is better than others." It was not that I thought I was better than anyone, but I had discovered that there was greatness in me. A greatness that did not have anything to do with what had happened to me in my past. It was all about me realizing that I was created with greatness in me. This world and the people in it will create roadblocks, sink holes, curve balls and whatever to distract you from the great person you are and the greatness you were designed to share with the world. You see, it is not just about you realizing you are great, but it is about using your greatness to build yourself up so that you have what it takes to build others up. It is a decision you have to make every single day that you will be intentional no matter what is happening. Les Brown is one of my favorite motivational speakers and he says, "It's not easy. It's hard changing your life, but don't stop running after your dreams (greatness). Rough times will come, but they are not here to stay. Do not say, I am having a bad day, but say that you are having a character-building day. As you go towards your future, realize that greatness is within you. If just one of you would envision yourselves that you are blessed and highly favored to reach your goals. If just one of you would capture the essence that you have greatness within you and a responsibility to manifest that greatness. That you can make others proud and touch many people's lives and the world will never be the same again, because you came their way. We all have a responsibility and an obligation to discover and operate in our greatness."

If you never successfully overcome challenging situations, how can you help others? For instance, how can you provide advice on how to rise above the pain of a miscarriage if you have never been pregnant? Let us take it one step forward, how can you inspire other women who have had a miscarriage if you have not worked through your own pain surrounding this? And this is the question I like to ask, "Would you rather be in a position where you can share sound advice on how to be and feel your greatness despite experiencing such a traumatic situation or would you rather be in a space where you are still demonstrating debilitating sadness because of what you went through?" We all have to make a choice on how much of our greatness we are willing to work for. A decision that nothing will dim your light. A decision to be the one. That is what it means to Be Intentional No Matter What - to make the decision that no matter what is happening, how much you are hurting, how embarrassing or how unfair situations are; you are going to still work on yourself and have the confidence to walk right into your greatness.

Your greatness should be so empowering that it makes others want to be around you. It should free you from your limitations so much so that it inspires others to want the same type of freedom in life.

The big question my clients ask me is "How?" Here are some simple steps that help me operate in my greatness.

1. **Daily Empowerment** – Just like you have to have the discipline to work out and have a nice muscular body, you have to also train your mind that you are great. You see it was not that I thought I was better than anyone when I finally decided to be great, but it was that I understood I was created to be great. I was not created to be sad and depressed. I love Larry Fitzgerald's quote on being great. He says, "You can never let anything distract you from your main goal of being great. Greatness is something nobody can ever take away from you, no matter what happens. So, I put all my energy and focus into my craft." My daily craft to empower my greatness involves reading my

bible, praying, learning a scripture relating to me, writing or reading positive affirmations, listening to motivational speakers. All of this help me to realize, the treasure that already exist in me was greatness given to me at birth, but I just needed to recognize this, have faith in what was inside me and work for my greatness to manifest.

2. **Eliminated People Who Secretly Wish for Our Demise** – We all know of people that we need to keep our distance from and who do not have our best interest in mind. However, have you ever thought about the people who you thought had your back or who should have your back, but they have demonstrated the following:
   a. People who sit back and watch you struggle without any type of moral or physical support.
   b. People who tell you that you do not have what it takes to reach your dreams.
   c. People who judge your character based on what you are going through. You know those Job type friends.

3. **Learn the Art of Not Caring** – When you have good intentions and you are doing the best that you can do, people will always have something to say about you or will not like you because you think you are better than others. You better hold your head up and shift your shoulders into King/Queen position. You and you alone know your story and your intentions. Continue to write your own story and work towards

your greatness. You have to understand that the judgement other people put on you is none of your business. So why get distracted by something that is not yours to own.

I literally exercise my right to be great everyday with these exercises. I am not perfect, my past is not perfect and my future likely will not be perfect, but I understand that I am fiercely and wonderfully made and have an obligation to Be Intentional No Matter What.

Heart to Heart Interviews

Selah - He that getteth wisdom loveth his own soul: he that keepeth understanding shall find good. Proverbs 19:8

We not only overcame this misfortune; we became better people. I realize now that because I faced the hurt and challenges head on, we were able to move into our purpose and live life to the fullest. Out of curiosity I wanted to know what other families had done to not only get over this near-death experience but to flourish and live a life that was powerful enough to even inspire others.

The next few pages consist of interviews collected from single Moms and Dads who have courageously taken on the challenges of single parenthood with grace and love. I am hoping that you fall within one of these categories and that the interview will provide you with the inspiration and guidance you need to be the best parent and person you can be for yourself and your children. I have categorized the single parent interviews into the following:

- **SINGLE MOMS WHO ARE DIVORCED OR SEPARATED**
- **SINGLE DADS WHO ARE DIVORCED OR SEPARATED**
- **SINGLE MOMS WHO ARE WIDOWS**
- **SINGLE DADS WHO ARE WIDOWS**
- **SINGLE MOMS NEVER MARRIED**
- **SINGLE DADS NEVER MARRIED** (unicorn situation that I had never even considered)

INTERVIEW WITH SINGLE DADS WHO ARE DIVORCED OR SEPARATED:

Richard!!!!

Daughter was five years old during separation
22 years old now
This whole experience with Kobe Bryant and Gigi has stirred something within me.
5 elements of a relationship with your child
Spiritual, physical, emotional financial &
I would talk to her 3 or 4 times a week.
One Christmas I flew to Frankfurt, Germany to pick up my daughter only to spend one full day with her due to the flight time and wanting to make sure she spent time with other family members.
When a relationship breaks...from the guys point of view the courts support the mother more so than the father when it comes to the emotional and financial aspects. Fathers love their children just as much as mothers, but most of the time the courts will side with the mother. This is frustrating and I do sit back and wonder, "How do you get guys to want to be involved?"
When I struggled with my daughter I asked my Mom, "Why do I put forth effort to have a relationship with my child when I am going to be the one to feel the lost?"
Most of the time the woman feels like their relationship with their child is co-dependent. They use the child as a pawn. And emotionally string the other parent along (the dad).
Fortunately, my ex was supportive, but I had to make sure to call her during my lunch time (US Eastern Standard Time) so I could talk to my daughter before her bedtime of 8pm (Germany Time). This was frustrating, but I did it out of respect for my daughter.
I am the one off. There are a lot of guys who do not want to go through this type of hassle & pain. They don't want to deal with the co-dependent relationship but just want a relationship with their child.

A lot of moms want a co-dependent relationship and fail to realize that the father does not always want this due to the pain associated with not having their child around all the time.

What is your favorite food? pizza

What is your favorite movie? There's too many ....Remember the Titans ...Dirty Dancing. That's (Dirty Dancing)actually a movie I use to watch with my daughter. She loves it!

Who is your favorite actor/actress? Denzel (actor). For the actress there are a tunnel of options ….can I get back with you on that

What is favorite sport? College football…because they have a passion for the game.

Who is your hero? My parents

What is your greatest fear? Dying….physically alone

What is your biggest challenge?
Overcoming my fear and finding someone

Have you tried dating sites?
I have thought about it, but there are too many options.

What was your biggest challenge?
Distance between my daughter and I

What is your current motivation?
My daughter

What was your motivation when your child was growing up? To make sure to break patterns that were happening ow both sides of the family. Probably more tied to generational stuff. My hope is that the court system realizes there are two parents that produce this child, and both should be able to influence the child. Children need both parents but need them differently at different phases of their life. I would say mothers are needed mostly at the beginning of the child's life and fathers at a later part of their life.

I believe the neutering of fathers from children's lives contribute to some homosexuality behaviors.

Relationship with children?
Great relationship. I am open book for my daughter and about her. My daughter is waiting for me to call all the time. When the teacher asked her what she got during her summer and holiday visits. The teacher advised me that my daughter said, "I can't tell you what I got from my Mom because I got so much from my Dad."

I remember when my church found out that my daughter was coming to stay with me during her high school years. I received some questions about whether I thought this was a good idea since she was a teenage girl. I was confident that having my daughter come stay with me was going to be a great experience for my daughter and that it would help her set a standard on how she should be treated as a young lady. I also wanted my daughter to understand what her American culture was like. For instance, in Germany, guys do not open doors for women. My daughter now expects for a guy to open the door for her.

Even though my daughter is a young lady now, the whole Kobe story has sparked some more thought to being a father to a young daughter. Like conversations about her Ghana boyfriend and how he should treat her.

Name one thing you would go back and change if you could.
A deeper relationship with my father. I got close to my father and 2 weeks later he dies. My brother died around 2002. WHY change it? It's tied with my fear of dying alone.

What gives you your inner strength? Richard: God! *Me: awesome.* Richard: Enjoying life and making the most of life. Renee Allen: Life with Richard": Making the most of life.

What advice would you give to a single parent on working towards keeping his family spiritually and emotionally close?
I would talk to her 3 or 4 times a week.

One Christmas I flew to Frankfurt, Germany to pick up my daughter only to spend one full day with her due to the flight time and wanting to make sure she spent time with other family members.

When a relationship breaks…from the guys point of view the courts support the mother more so than the father when it comes to the emotional and financial aspects. Fathers love their children just as much as mothers, but most of the time the courts will side with the mother. This is frustrating and I do sit back and wonder, "How do you get guys to want to be involved?"

When I struggled with my daughter, I asked my Mom, "Why do I put forth effort to have a relationship with my child when I am going to be the one to feel the lost?"

Most of the time the woman feels like their relationship with their child is co-dependent. They use the child as a pawn. And emotionally string the other parent along (the dad).

Fortunately, my ex was supportive, but I had to make sure to call her during my lunch time (US Eastern Standard Time) so I could talk to my daughter before her bedtime of 8pm (Germany Time). This was frustrating, but I did it out of respect for my daughter.

I am the one off. There are a lot of guys who do not want to go through this type of hassle & pain. They don't want to deal with the co-dependent relationship but just want a relationship with their child.

A lot of moms want a co-dependent relationship and fail to realize that the father does not always want this due to the pain associated with not having their child around all the time.

Why do you think you are/were successful as a single parent?
Because I did not want to fail my child. I have one child and the strength I get from God helps me to stay focus. This situation (being there for your child when they are little/young) is short term but the results with be for a lifetime. What kind of positive impact? What legacy…your

child and what you put into them is the legacy that carries on. If you do not teach them when they are young, then when will you do it?

INTERVIEW WITH SINGLE DADS WHO ARE WIDOWS:
Joe 57
What is your favorite food? *Don't have a particular favorite....my palate...have to go with a southern dish....since that is the way I was raised. So, yes soul food.*

What is your favorite movie? *Hmmm...action movie...specific ....I recently watched the Harry Potter series. After all these years it's been out.*

Who is your favorite actor/actress? *Denzel...he has a wide range / now that's a good one...Cicely Tyson...I can remember her when growing up.*

What is your favorite sport? *Football...Redskins because my nephew played with them....now it is Green Bay.*

Who is your hero? *Mom....pillar of strength*

What is your greatest fear? *I don't think I really have one. I would say, "not being in control." More like the fear of the unknown. I like to have some type of plan.*

What is your biggest challenge?
Getting Trey, my son, back to normalcy. Taking over after losing my wife and him losing his Mom. And me not knowing the load a mother takes on. I should have known more of what was going on....more involved...more in tune...forward leaning. You know how guys have the mentality of "bringing home the bacon." Having the qualities of a homemaker like a mother is important for guys to have also. How to be a nurturer. With my wife, she would know the right question to ask. I only knew to ask, "What is wrong?" and respond with "Nothing is

wrong with you." My tone ....my body language caused my son to shut down. I like the energy my wife brought to our home and I wish I had that. For 4 years, I have been trying to figure it out. Now, I have to figure out our family values and traditions (i.e., quality time....sitting around table).

I read a book called Breast Cancer Husband: How to Help Your Wife (and Yourself) During Diagnosis, Treatment and Beyond, a book that helps you in case there is no cure for your wife was very helpful. What I got out of it is that you are not in this alone. "All you have to do is ask" that is what Dina use to say. She would say, "you don't have to do this by yourself." I felt like everything was my responsibility. There were a whole lot of other things like people bringing food over or people visiting to lift her spirits. I get what your book is about. There are a lot of moving parts.

You know, I really want them (my children) to know this is their home. When my Mom use to ask about me coming home, I did not understand at the time why she was asking me to come home so much. I finally got this after my wife died. I understood why she was so adamant about me coming home more. I want my kids to know that this is their home and spiritually this is their home.

I remember bringing my Mom to come visit me after my wife died. I took her to Urgent Care the same day she arrived and Urgent Care advised they could not do anything for her. Urgent Care advise me to take her to the emergency room. I took her over to the ER and was advised to get her to her family doctor as soon as possible. I was not aware that the ER doctor and her family doctor where under strict instructions not to let me know what was wrong with Mom. My Mother protected me from knowing what was wrong with her, because of my wife's passing. That is a mother's protection and her love to the end. She passed away not too long after I got her back home.

What was your biggest challenge?

A mental challenge was and to some degree still is my biggest challenge. I find it hard to be motivated and positive. I have a facade of being positive, but I am not as motivated. 2025 is retirement and all my plans of retiring with my wife will not happen. All our dreams have faded. Retiring makes me think about the first week after my wife passed. TJ said, "are we going to move now" And in my mind I wanted to quit work and just leave, but my son asked to finish high school. I immediately thought about when I was in Okinawa and our two older sons were in high school…one in 12th & one in 11th, and I was ready to leave Okinawa. However, I listened to my wife about allowing the boys to finish out high school with their friends and decided to stay. I took this same forward leaning and thought about what TJ was asking. I wanted to escape especially since I did not have a family/nucleus to help me in Virginia. I am happy that I did so that my son could finish school. It had always been in my mind to pack up and go. It was also better financially to stay put.

Holidays, birthday's …are not the same anymore. This year was the hardest. I was just not in the Christmas spirit. My son was away to college and I did not feel like putting up a tree. I eventually put the tree up and decorated with ornaments TJ made when he was little. Put white boxes under the tree…but no lights on the Christmas tree. "Chuckle" I will get the lights on eventually.

What is your current motivation?
Maintaining motivation to keep dreaming. Take the demotivation to get to a new place. I am learning to be motivated. I am happy…but not that type of happy I use to get when I come home and laid on her lap, have her rub my head or here her say, "gone Joe".

What was your motivation when your children were growing up? Make sure my children felt loved.

How old are your children? *19, 32, 35*

How old were they when your spouse passed away? *15, 28, 31 on Dec 26th*

Relationship with children? *Father – son relationship*

Name one thing you would go back and change if you could.
I cannot say I would change anything. Proverbs 3:5-6. The reason why all this happened. My family is who we are because of what we went through. We failed, we were humbled; we got back up and we are succeeding.

What gives you your inner strength? *Knowing God …even though I haven't been to church in 6mos. I mean as black folks we always fall back to God. I do not put my trust in God.*

Why do you think you are/were successful as a single parent? *'Silence' When you put God first…..even though I want to quit…I know I can't quit. People need you; it is just like when you have a business. Also, realizing the inner strength you have. It has been four years and I have gotten better. I know I can find another woman, but I don't want to share what my wife and I built together. Emotionally I am in a good place. It's good that I don't have to answer to anyone. A little chuckle and a repeat of what some woman has asked him - "What do you mean where I have been" Yes, I don't want to be alone. I do think about being alone, but I am good right now.*
You might get set back but it is not the end of world…but there is something inside of you that will not let you quit.
Now, it is very important and please write "utilize your resources…therapy/counseling/people you can trust…..opening yourself up ….find someone who will listen…the only thing I wanted was for someone to listen and not feel obligated to do anything, but simply having someone that will just listen. It is also helpful to have friends that do not necessarily have to call you all the time but are there when you need them. They are friends that can simply look at you and know something is not right and will tell you.

I also have a journal and that has been very helpful too.

What advice would you give to a single parent on working towards keeping his little family spiritually and emotionally close?

First, I had to first make sure I was emotionally healthy. I am glad I had resources from work for myself and my son, because it opened up my eyes to how important getting counseling is to help you get over something so traumatizing. I didn't find out that I was not coping well with my wife's death until I started going to my job counseling sessions by myself. However, when I took my son, I really started to see through his eyes that I was not handling the situation very well. My son could only get a certain amount of sessions. Due to the job only allowing so many sessions for my son, I decided to reach out to the Veterans Affairs (VA) for help.

People say take it to the alter and have faith, and that's fine, but God place these services & people in my life to help put me on the track that enabled me to help my son who was only 15. Our other two sons where grown so they had the ability to cope better with their Mother's death. Finding that emotional health help me to have a stronger faith and it all circled back around to my wife convincing me to have a Godly and fatherly relationship with my sons. I worked on my emotional self because I needed to take my son to get help. I started attending church more. It was helpful to my son because this was his church family. Right now, I don't participate in church too much, but I am grateful for the church's support.

Don't get me wrong I still grieve, because of remembering all the holidays, anniversaries, it saddens me. Tony was just going to high school and I had to help him cope with this somehow.

I found out that my unhealthiness in dealing with my wife's death was causing my son to shut down. I also had to open up to receive the help. Now, I learn something. You can tell the ones (people) that are serious about being there for you. People say, "If you need any help call me." Tony said, "I should not have to call you. You know what I am going through." I like when people would show up and ring the doorbell with an entire meal…AN ENTIRE MEAL!

Every day I would ask my son, "have you did your work and he would say, "yes." Only for me to find out that he was failing everything. I have to credit Ellen, my friend, for helping TJ. She came up with a plan for me to bring him over to do his homework at her house and it worked. It took TJ away from the house right after school and away from the tension I was creating. So, I would pick him up after school and take him over to Ellen's house. You know that song by Fred Hyman, "Be a fence all around me," well that's what was happening between the church, meals delivered and Ellen.

I would say you have to be emotionally healthy. My wife always kept her finger on TJ's pulse. The older kids it stung but they had coping skills to deal with it.

But, oh, my goodness, I did not see myself through my own eyes until someone said something to me. You know the best way for me to explain this I that I just had my closet redone because the shelves fell. I went out and bought some racks and was content with that. Then I decided to let someone come and install the racks and organize the closet for me. The installer came out and took some before pictures. When the work was completed, I looked at my before pictures and it was actually in disarray. You see the before and after pictures remind me that getting help is sometimes better for you. Now my closet is organized. Then I recognized that both of my closets were disorganized so had that one organized too. You might think your closet/your mind is organized but take a before and after picture to make sure. I was just doing things to ease the pain, but now I have fallen in tune with myself.

This was so powerful that I had comment. I asked Mr. Tony, "do you realized that you just told a story that sums up what you have been saying while answering this question." Here is what I got from this that was such a blessing to my soul – Life is going to happen to all of us, but you do not have to face everything alone. It takes a village! So, the next time you want to give up. The next time you do not know how you

are going to make it – "don't resist help but do the exact opposite and reach out to the experts (i.e., church, counseling, friends).
I never questioned the spiritual part of my wife's deaf. A lot of people ask why I am not mad, and I am just so grateful that she is not suffering anymore. I was telling my brother about a recurring dream I kept having about my wife leaving. She would say, "I am leaving you."

INTERVIEW WITH SINGLE DADS NEVER MARRIED:
Andy 32

How old are your children?
2 on May 10th

What is your favorite food?
I eat about everything …but I would say salmon

What is your favorite movie?
Ah man. Huh! Probably have to say..my all-time favorite the original Lion King

Who is your favorite actor/actress?
Denzel/Samuel L Jackson   Angela Basset/Nia Long

What is your favorite sport?
Well, I played football in college.

Who is your hero?
My Dad

What is your greatest fear?
Something happening to the boys while they are with their mom.

What is your biggest challenge?

Just making sure I am making enough to take care of them & myself.

What was your biggest challenge? *Try to figure how to handle it all, because I was very clear to the kids Mom that we were not together, and I feel like she got pregnant to try to trap me.*

What is your current motivation? *Teaching them to be best that they can. I definitely want to raise them to be good people.*

What was your motivation when your children were growing up?
They are only one now. So.... (Me....I gotcha...ok, next question)

Relationship with children?
It is fun...but they still know I am Dad ....and they already know when my tone changes to "serious Dad."

Name one thing you would go back and change if you could.
Who their Mom is.

What gives you your inner strength?
As far as the boys...each night they fall asleep while I am reading to them and seeing them resting and safe means the world to me.

Why do you think you are/were successful as a single parent?
Because of my support system ......everyone in my immediate circle has helped out in so many ways.

INTERVIEW WITH SINGLE MOMS WHO ARE DIVORCED OR SEPARATED:
Maria age 51.

How old are your children?
20, 19, & 14

What is your biggest challenge?
I would say balancing. You are playing two roles – provider and nurturer. Who is your back up? "Why is that" Because they had their own family to worry about and they don't have time. I have to always have my children ready for whatever comes their way. Both of the girls work and save their money or help buy groceries. Their mentality is different, and they feel pressured to have their stuff together.

What was your biggest challenge?
When your children are growing your challenges changes, because the demands are different at each age. When they were younger, I was more concerned with nurturing them (i.e., Making it to a soccer game and PTA meetings). When they got older it became more of a financial challenge. (now I have to make sure they are prepared for life). If I had worked more when they were little, my kids would not have the self-confidence they have now.
It was hard because I gave up so much to my marriage and this guy just walked out on his family. It makes me sad for the kids, but honestly, I am sadder that I gave up so much for my marriage for it to just die.

What is your current motivation?
My priority is to make sure I can provide for them.

What was your motivation when your children were growing up?
Make sure my children felt loved. Being a single Mom has been stressful but rewarding.

Relationship with children?
Different with my son, because I cannot raise a man. So, I looked for an outsource like "my Brother's keeper". With my daughters, it was more in source guidance and much easier.

Name one thing you would go back and change if you could.
I cannot say I would. My family is who we are because of what we went through. We failed, we were humbled; we got back up and we are succeeding.

What gives you your inner strength?
Being the matriarch for my family. I told God I want to be the role model to teach my children to be resilient and want to serve the community.

Why do you think you are/were successful as a single parent?
I would say because I have great kids who are humbled. Like for Christmas sometimes they only get a few gifts and they are grateful for it. They do not act entitled. My children show me that I have been successful.

What advice would you give to a single parent on working towards keeping her family spiritually and emotionally close?
Be the example. You can tell your kids whatever you want but you have to be the example.

INTERVIEW WITH SINGLE MOMS WHO ARE DIVORCED OR SEPARATED:
Brandi age 60

How old are your children?
26 & 30

What is your favorite food?
Chicken salad

What is your favorite movie?
I don't know if I have a favorite movie, but I enjoy love stories.

Who is your favorite actor/actress?
Denzel (actor). Angela Basset.

What is favorite sport?
Basketball

Who is your hero?
Dad

What is your greatest fear? *Fear that I will not be around to see my grandchildren grow up. Or see my children fulfilled their dreams.*

What is your biggest challenge? *Facing retirement and knowing that I still need to work to compensate my retirement. Trying to close out my 30 years. I want to do something different.*

What was your biggest challenge? *Trying to decide if I was going to stay in the house or go get apartment. Then I started thinking that I wanted to leave something for my kids. So, I started getting my finances right and did what I had to do to stay in my house.*

What is your current motivation? *Retire and see what's next for me I life. I have to find how to make a difference. I have to discover that next chapter in my life*

What was your motivation when your children were growing up? *To be a good parent. Be a role model for my parent. To provide a Christine foundation for my children so that they would have faith and trust in God even after they were grown.....Wanted them* to both go to college and to get an education and be successful. I wanted to let them know how important that was.

Relationship with children? *Proud of my children. They really stuck by me. My daughter and I are really close. She looks out for me and makes sure that I am ok. My daughter even stays on my son about checking on me.*

Name one thing you would go back and change if you could. *I can't think of anything. I made sure I do not put their dad down or discuss how he did me. I probably would have encouraged them to talk to their dad back when we divorced, because I have heard them say, "he has never apologized to us." I would have encouraged my ex to talk to my kids and explain what was going on but didn't want anything to do with him. I think to some degree, separations and divorces impact adult kids more so than smaller kids, because they understand what is happening. It is hard for the children, because they have to change the way they do things. Or the family structure, or lack thereof, makes things challenging. For instance, my ex came over to see my daughter while she was home and he mention that he was really concerned about being able to take his granddaughter to get ice cream or just simply seeing the grand baby. My daughter asked why he felt that way and my ex said because our son hardly spends time with him. My daughter advised my ex-husband to talk to our son. If we were together this would not have even been an issue.*

What gives you your inner strength? *My faith. I could tell you that being a pastor wife and going through this was not easy. The shame that you endure has caused some 1st Ladies to lose their mind.*

Why do you think you are/were successful as a single parent? *I didn't give up ad I continued to trust in God. And I moved forward and heard God say , "it was not going to always be this way. I went from having nothing…from borrower to lender. I had to have faith in myself and trust God.*

INTERVIEW WITH SINGLE MOMS WHO ARE WIDOWS:
Terri 65

How old are your children?
44, 43, 41, 40, 38

What is your favorite food?
Bake chicken

What is your favorite movie?
No favorite movie, but I like CSI type stories.

Who is your favorite actor/actress?
Tyler Perry

What is your favorite sport?
Bingo

Who is your hero?
Ain't but one hero for everybody – God

What is your greatest fear?
Water… I can't swim.

What is your biggest challenge?
Keeping the children together and teaching them to get along.

What was your biggest challenge? *When they were growing up, I was making sure I made enough money to take care of them*

What is your current motivation?
Staying healthy

What was your motivation when your children were growing up?
Taking care of them

Relationship with children? *Mmmh! Some distance with some of my children and some I am close with. Try to be there friend and take one day at a time. Try to get along with them because everybody is different.*

Name one thing you would go back and change if you could.
Nothing I can think of

What gives you your inner strength?
God does

Why do you think you are/were successful as a single parent? *I don't think I was successful enough. I did my best and thank God it turned out ok.*

INTERVIEW WITH SINGLE MOMS NEVER MARRIED:
Noel 35

How old are your children?
16

What is your favorite food?
Italian food

What is your favorite movie?
Princess Bride

Who is your favorite actor?
Denzel

Who is your favorite actress?
Do I have one?......that will be tougher to pinpoint.

What is your favorite sport?
Softball

Who is your hero? *Not one in particular, but I do have a type of hero. Women who are very strong, have overcome obstacles...those women who have made a way out of no way. Their way has not been easy, but they have achieved a lot.*

What is your greatest fear? *Not preparing my son for life before I transition. I want to make sure he is prepared for life when I am no longer here for him.*

What is your biggest challenge? *Time management! I am in school and I am really working on being able to commit myself to do well at everything I do. Having balance. Which means spending time at home, having time for school and having time for myself.*

What was your biggest challenge? *In AJ's younger years...finance & support system. I do not have family in the area so figuring out how to pick him up from daycare at a certain time was sometimes challenging. Sometimes, I would have to take him back to the office. For finances, kids are expensive and now that I look back, I wish I had spent less. Being young spending on the wrong things.* **Me:** *Would you contribute finance being the biggest challenge because you spent too much when you were young or was it a challenge because you were a single Mom.* **Noel:** *I believe it was due to the combination of both over the years.*

What is your current motivation? *I would say ...since NJ is a little bit older...he recognizes what he has to do. So, now...I am starting to insert myself into more things. I want to feed who I am and coming to better idea of who I want to be.*

What was your motivation when your children were growing up? *Not to kill him! You want to do everything right. I want to raise a son who had a lot of love and exposure to make him as centered a kid as possible.*

Relationship with children? *Man, you know those teenage years...I was a good kid. You want to give them freedom to express themselves, but I do remind him that he is not grown. It's a challenge because you want to let your child autonomy, but the world doesn't see you for who you really are. The world may see you as 21, but you are only 13. No texting or receiving text of naked pictures....be mindful.*

Name one thing you would go back and change if you could. *Being more assertive and speaking up to my son's father. I was not very confident in myself. I was not getting what I wanted for NJ & myself and should have spoken up.*

What gives you your inner strength? *Knowing all the strong women before me in my family. Things came to me easily. I could quickly problem solve almost anything, but when you are grown it doesn't always happen. Just because you want positive to happen does not mean positive will happen.*

Why do you think you are/were successful as a single parent? *Man..all the times I screwed up. Sometimes you have to learn the hard way. I am grateful for my connections/relationships. They have help me figure out how to do a lot. I am able to garner advice from others who have gone through something similar. So, combination of learning* the hard way & having a tribe. You need challenges to help you grow and help others.

INTERVIEW WITH SINGLE MOMS THAT HAVE REMARRIED:
The Superwoman Herself: AJ 70

How old are your children?
50, 49, 47, 43

What is your favorite food?
Fried chicken

What is your favorite movie?
Anything by Tyler Perry

Who is your favorite actor/actress?
I just said anything Tyler Perry/Madea

What is your favorite sport?
Don't really have one

Who is your hero?
My Mom

What is your greatest fear? *I really didn't have one. My thing was that raising the kids as a single Mom, I wanted the kids to do better than me. I want them to thrive regardless of what happened to them -married, divorced, never married — I wanted to make sure they could live a life that they loved regardless of anyone else being there for them or not. I wanted them to go to school and establish a life for themselves where they could be independent and not have their quality of life to be dictated by someone else.*

What is your biggest challenge? *Raising 4 kids alone. Wanted them not to be in trouble. Just because you are single doesn't mean you have to be on welfare. I also wanted to make sure I did not raise kids who were in trouble with the law. You know people look at your children and expect them to get in trouble and do all kinds of crazy stuff just because you are raising them by yourself. When you are a single parent you don't need to be your child's friend. They got their friends and I have mind.*

What was your biggest challenge? *I really don't have any challenges. I have overcome all my challenges and happy with how I raised my kids.*

What is your current motivation? *I finally bought my home and I have a lot to do so I have the home ready and comfortable like I want once I retire.*

What was your motivation when your children were growing up? *Well, what was really motivating was how well they were achieving in school. They were good kids who listened and always wanted something out of life.* **Laughter:** *Probably because they knew I would get them back in line with a good spanking.*

Relationship with children? Great. We are fine! We all love each other and want the best for each other. Singing....*We are one big happy family*

Name one thing you would go back and change if you could? *If I could, I would have gotten my education first and then I would have gotten married around 30. Back when I was growing up, older people didn't motivate you to go to school and set up a good life for yourself. The only thing they use to say is, "keep your dress down." I can remember thinking, "what does that mean." And if you got pregnant in high school you had to quit school.*

What advice would you advise to a single parent on working towards keeping his/her family close: *To keep the kids close - communicate & motivate them to do better than you. Sometimes, you have to force /push them to go on and do something bigger because they are too young to understand. My youngest daughter actually received a scholarship to play ball in college, but she did not take it because she thought it would be a waste of time to play in college since the professional women's basketball teams did not exist back then. I tried everything to convince her but was unsuccessful and now there are professional women teams. This is why I say, you have to push them to do somethings whether they think they should be doing it or not. My daughter thought she was going to stay home and work some job that was paying her like $200 week. I told her she did not have to play basketball, but she was going to school. You see I understood enough to know that working a job like this was only going to have her struggling for the rest of her life. I did not want this. So, I told her she was going to school and now she is married and doing very well for herself.*
I would also say, remind your kids not to listen to other kids on what they can and cannot do, because people will attempt to discourage your children from doing something great just because they do not have the desire to be something great or think it is too hard.

What gives you your inner strength? *Well, knowing that the kids are all self-sufficient and really all I have to provide is nothing more than moral support. Just knowing they are achieved and still are achievers.*

Why do you think you are/were successful as a single parent? *Well, I feel like I was successful because I always made sure the kids had before I had. It didn't matter whether I had anything as long as they had what they needed and were happy.*

How was your relationship with the children's Dad? *We never had a relationship because I feel like he could have done more. Now, he is older and regretting it. He was not there for them because he did not think I had the fortitude and capability to make it on my own, but I did. Now, when I see him, I am still cordial. I speak and keep going.*

INTERVIEW WITH SINGLE MOMS THAT HAVE FINALLY MARRIED:
<u>Eva Age 38</u>

How old are your children?
17, 10, 6, 2

How long were you single before getting married?
7yrs

What is your favorite food?
Fried fish

What is your favorite movie?
The Color Purple

Who is your favorite actor/actress?
Will Smith/Angela Basset

What is your favorite sport?
Basketball. I like to watch gymnastics. I was cheerleader.

Who is your hero?
My Dad!

What is your greatest fear?
Letting my girls down whichever way ….disappointing them.

What is your biggest challenge? *Balance…not losing myself in being a good mother…you give up a lot to be a mother….you wake up one day and wonder what happened to accomplishing my dreams.*

What was your biggest challenge? *Seems harder now….easier to raise one child single than raising 4 kids married….even though I had less money, I feel that I had more energy and time. Feeling like you had to prove yourself. Childcare was a challenge. Working 80 hours a week. College, work and taking care of my child was a lot.*

What is your current motivation?
Definitely, the girls. Desire to live up to my potential.

What was your motivation when your children were growing up? *Dee-Dee. She really was. I had a t-shirt made with her baby picture on it that said, "you are my motivation." She was my motivation. I wanted to give her the life I had and more. Dee-Dee sleeps in the shirt now. Children change the purpose of life and help you to be less selfish.*

Relationship with children?
I have a great relationship with them. Our relationship is very open, fun, and loving.

Name one thing you would go back and change if you could. *"laughter" from Eva and then she says, I use to say nothing, but I would have to say I would be more confident. I would trust myself and go harder.*

What gives you your inner strength?

Hmmm…God…my faith…knowing that he creates my path and my destiny. I just have to have the courage to walk it out.

Why do you think you are/were successful as a single parent?

I think I was successful as a single parent because my dad and mom instill core values. My parents grew up I southern Mississippi…where life is not easy. My dad uses to say ."piss poor planning on your part does not create an emergency for me. "never let them see you sweat." My dad was in the military. He was my hero. My senior year I high school my dad ruptured his spleen playing basketball, and through this mishap he found out he had cancer. I was like daddy's girl and this whole experience opened my eyes. My dad never let anyone know he had cancer. He had a great attitude and work ethic. He still went to the gym, went to work, took care of the family. Because he kept going with normal activities, I didn't see him as being sick. I mean we knew he was sick, but he did not stop being who he was because of the illness. He masked the sickness. Then one thanksgiving he was in Maryland and could not talk to us because he was so sick. This is when I realized he was really sick. One day when I was crying about breaking up with my fiancée my father said, "get yourself together! I have already told you no one is going to care for you like you will care for yourself. He said you have already given all you can to the relationship and given him enough time. Now, pick yourself up and carry on. He said, when your body is weak you have to be strong in your mind." It was very challenging, but my father's advice helped me to move forward, work hard and to not rely on others. I hope I am passing these same core values on to my children.

INTERVIEW WITH SINGLE MOMS THAT HAVE FINALLY MARRIED:
Ethel 62 years old

What is your favorite food?
Use to be spaghetti, but don't know if I have one since I cut beef out of my diet.

What is your favorite movie?
Cinderella with Brandi

Who is your favorite actor/actress?
Cicely Tyson

What is favorite sport?
Biking

Who is your hero?
My Dad and Mom. My Mom is my shero! And Dad was

What is your greatest fear?
One of my kids dying before me

How old are your children?
22 27 & 32

How old were your children when you became a single Mom?
I was 30.

What is your biggest challenge?
Hoping that they see they need an education. Find a way to build their own dreams. Not having to work a 9-5 but having their own business.

What was your biggest challenge? *Trying to make more money to provide for my kids.*

What is your current motivation? *Well, I have a small business and want to grow it so they can join in if they want. I am working to leave a legacy for my children.*

What was your motivation when your children were growing up?
Keeping them fed. Making sure they stayed out of trouble and keep them out of the streets. I wanted to see them go off to school and do something technical.

Relationship with children?
It's good. I really focus on making sure I stay connected with all of them. My youngest one calls a lot. I facetime with daughter so I can see my grandkids almost every day. My middle son doesn't call as much but does stay in touch. So, I have a pretty relationship with all my kids.

Name one thing you would go back and change if you could. *The things with how I spent my cash and what I spent my cash on. The credit does take a hit when you are doing whatever you can to provide for your children all by yourself, especially if you want to do avoid doing anything illegal.*

What gives you your inner strength?
Relationship with God. Not perfect…but just being honest and trusting Him.

Why do you think you are/were successful as a single parent? *One of the things I notice with the father not being involved is that I had a father who encourage me to be my best. With me having a father and knowing what he expected from me. I knew I could not be* *a father, but I at least internalized what my father wanted and expected and so I expected the same from my children.*

What is your biggest challenge?
I would say balancing. You are playing two roles – provider and nurturer. Who is your back up? "Why is that" Because they had their own family to worry about and they don't have time. I have to always have my children ready for whatever comes their way. Both of the girls work and save their money or help buy groceries. Their mentality is different, and they feel pressured to have their stuff together.

What was your biggest challenge?
When your children are growing your challenges changes because the demands are different at each age. When they were younger, I was more concerned with nurturing them (i.e., Making it to a soccer game and PTA meetings). When they got older it became more of a financial challenge. (now I have to make sure they are prepared for life). If I had worked more when they were little, my kids would not have the self-confidence they have now.

What is your current motivation?
My priority is to make sure I can provide for them.

What was your motivation when your children were growing up?
Make sure my children felt loved. Being a single Mom has been stressful but rewarding.

Relationship with children?
Different with my son because I cannot raise a man. So, I looked for an outside source like an organization called "My Brother's Keeper." With my daughters, it was more in source guidance and much easier.

It was hard because I gave up so much to my marriage and this guy just walked out on his family. It makes me sad for the kids, but honestly, I am sadder that I gave up so much for my marriage for it to just die.

Name one thing you would go back and change if you could.
I cannot say I would. My family is who we are because of what we went through. We failed, we were humbled; we got back up and we are succeeding.

What gives you your inner strength?
God

Why do you think you are/were successful as a single parent?
I worked hard and stayed on top of my children to make sure they did not get locked up and always encouraged them to get an education so they could do better than me.

I was so blessed and inspired by these powerful men and women. The stories were a blessing in disguise. I am tremendously grateful that they allowed a glimpse of what it was like to be a single parent and even more motivated by their courage and encourage other single parents. The time I spent with these parents helped me to realize that God and the universe endows us with power to overcome and live a life of abundance. Therefore, every single challenge must be faced with a positive and hopeful attitude with the understanding that the challenge is necessary if we are to live out our true purpose. "Continue to do good in the spite of what you are going through." It may be painful and seem unfair, but I am a living witness that good things will start happening for you.

Selah Inspiration Resources

1. **Be Intentional *No Matter What* Summit YouTube Channel:**
   The 2021 Be Intentional No Matter What Summit channel is Exactly What You Need Right Now! This is going to be a life changing experience that will help you figure out what strategy to take to get the results you want in life for you and your family. 2021 is the year to discover how to develop meaningful relationships, healthier lifestyles, and better finances. I have invited some experts on my YouTube channel to share strategies, experiences, knowledge and wisdom with you during the 2021 to help you live a life of confidence and abundance like I have been able to do.

2. **Be Intentional *No Matter What* Budget Spreadsheet Template:**
   Develop and Track Your Budget: I developed an excel spreadsheet that allowed me to enter my monthly income and expenses to track my net income for the month. I used this spreadsheet to ensure I had a visual of what bills I had to pay, when my bills were due, what extra money I had to save. This strategy ensured I stayed within my budget and eventually resulted in all my bills being paid off. I updated this spreadsheet on a weekly basis. This spreadsheet, along with prayer, was the foundation for my credit score increasing by 200 points in 10 months.

3. **Be Intentional *No Matter What* Understanding Your Strengths Test:**

   During each phase of my bouncing back, I made sure to do some self-introspection to improve myself and to give myself a chance at living the best version of my life. It is important to understand your strengths, because then you will understand how to become the best version of yourself. Your strengths are recurring patterns of thoughts, decisions, actions, and feelings that reveal foundational traits about you. If you are interested in understanding some of your core strengths, take the Strengths test offered on my website. You gain the following from taking the test:

   a. *You feel natural at using and developing your ability.*
   b. *You get positive energy when using your strengths.*
   c. *Others also perceive it as your strength.*
   d. *It goes along with your values and understanding of a strength.*
   e. *It satisfies your inner needs.*

4. ***Be Intentional No Matter What* Newsletter**
   The *Be Intentional Newsletter* will provide information and educational material relevant to each month. The newsletter will provide current events, tips and quotes that will inspire you to live your best life. Great articles to read each month on relationship building, finances and healthy living.

5. ***Be Intentional No Matter What* Mini-Online course:**
   This course is designed to jump start your journey to living your best life. You will discover how to be unapologetically you and how to overcome any obstacle.

A workbook, transformational lessons, interviews with other life coaches pertaining to the weekly lessons, affirmation cards to provide the foundation you need to bounce back when life happens. This course will help you discover the strategies and techniques to utilize in motivating yourself and others. If you are serious about living your best life and becoming the best version of yourself then you will want to invest in this course.

6. *Be Intentional No Matter What* **Keynote Speaker**:
Are you looking to inspire the people at your company, a team of people or yourself? I can help you grow your business, improve relationships, develop positive attitudes, become healthy achieve financial prosperity and simply enjoy life more. If you are serious about being the best version of yourself, want to inspire students to be their best, motivate church members, build up your company's team, or maximize all your organization's strengths, I am available. I specialize in providing customized presentation for any occasion.

To sign-up for these programs and learn of other opportunities, please visit my website: www.SelahInspiration.com

66 Day Challenge

Selah - Being confident of this very thing, that he which hath begun a good work in you will perform it until the day of Jesus Christ... Philippians 1:6

Studies shows that it takes 66 to 365 days for a new behavior to become automatic. Here are 66 scriptures I used to completely transform my thought process and stay focused. Take a moment to speak this wisdom out loud. Remind yourself who you are and to whom you belong and what has already been accomplished in your life. Trust that He who began a good work in your life will indeed complete it. In about two months, you will develop a habit that will help you reach your dreams and live a life of abundance.

66 Days of Inspiration:

Jeremiah 29:11 - For I know the thoughts that I think toward you, saith the LORD, thoughts of peace, and not of evil, to give you an expected end.

Joshua 1:9 – Have not I commanded thee? Be strong and of a good courage; be not afraid, neither be thou dismayed: for the Lord thy God is with thee whithersoever thou goest.

Psalms 1:1-2 - He that dwelleth in the secret place of the most High shall abide under the shadow of the Almighty. I will say of the LORD, He is my refuge and my fortress: my God; in him will I trust.

Psalm 1:3 - And he shall be like a tree planted by the rivers of water, that bringeth forth his fruit in his season; his leaf also shall not wither; and whatsoever he doeth shall prosper.

I Corinthians 13:4-8 - Charity suffereth long, [and] is kind; charity envieth not; charity vaunteth not itself, is not puffed up, Doth not behave itself unseemly, seeketh not her own, is not easily provoked, thinketh no evil; Rejoiceth not in iniquity, but rejoiceth in the truth; Beareth all things, believeth all things, hopeth all things, endureth all things. Charity never faileth: but whether [there be] prophecies, they shall fail; whether [there be] tongues, they shall cease; whether [there be] knowledge, it shall vanish away.

1 John 4:18 - There is no fear in love; but perfect love casteth out fear: because fear hath torment. He that feareth is not made perfect in love.

1 Corinthians 13:1-13 - Though I speak with the tongues of men and of angels, and have not charity, I am become [as] sounding brass, or a tinkling cymbal.

1 Corinthians 13:13 - And now abideth faith, hope, charity, these three; but the greatest of these [is] charity.

John 1:5 - The light shines in the darkness, and the darkness has not overcome it.

Romans 8:37 No, in all these things we are more than conquerors through him who loved us.

1 John 4:4 You, dear children, are from God and have overcome them, because the one who is in you.

Isaiah 43:1-3 Do not fear, for I have redeemed you; I have called you by name, you are mine. When you pass through the waters, I will be with you; and through the rivers, they shall not overwhelm you; when you walk through fire you shall not be burned, and the flame shall not consume you. For I am the Lord you God, the Holy One of Israel, your Savior.

Luke 12:25-26 Who of you by worrying can add a single hour to your life[a]? 26 Since you cannot do this very little thing, why do you worry about the rest?

John 14:27 Peace I leave with you; my peace I give you. I do not give to you as the world gives. Do not let your hearts be troubled and do not be afraid.

Psalm 34:4 I sought the Lord, and he answered me, and delivered me from all my fears.

Psalm 27: 1-3 The LORD is my light and my salvation whom shall I fear? The LORD is the stronghold of my life—of whom shall I be afraid? When the wicked advance against me to devour me, it is my enemies and my foes who will stumble and fall. Though an army besiege me, my heart will not fear; though war break out against me, even then I will be confident.

2 Timothy 1:7 For God did not give us a spirit of timidity, but a spirit of power, of love and of self-discipline.

Psalm 138:3 When I called, you answered me; you made me bold and stouthearted.

Psalm 16:8 I have set the Lord always before me. Because he is at my right hand, I will not be shaken.

Psalm 62:1-2 My soul finds rest in God alone; my salvation comes from him. He alone is my rock and my salvation; he is my fortress; I will never be shaken.

Psalm 112: 1, 7-8 Praise the Lord! Happy are those who fear the Lord. They are not afraid of evil tidings; their hearts are firm, secure in the Lord. Their hearts are steady, they will not be afraid.

2 Corinthians 12:9 My grace is sufficient for you, for my power is made perfect in weakness.

Philippians 4: 12-13 I know what it is to be in need, and I know what it is to have plenty. I have learned the secret of being content in any and every situation . . . . I can do everything through him who gives me strength.

2 Thessalonians 3:3 But the Lord is faithful, and he will strengthen and protect you from the evil one.

Isaiah 40:29 He gives power to the weak and strength to the powerless.

1 Peter 5: 10 And the God of all grace, who called you to his eternal glory in Christ, after you have suffered a little while, will himself restore you and make you strong, firm and steadfast.

Hebrews 4:16 For we do not have a high priest who is unable to sympathize with our weaknesses, but we have one who in every respect has been tested as we are, yet without sin. Let us therefore approach the throne of grace with boldness, so that we may receive mercy and find grace to help in time of need.

Deuteronomy 31:6,8 Be strong and bold; have no fear or dread of them, because it is the Lord your God who goes before you. He will be with you; he will not fail you or forsake you. Do not fear or be dismayed.

2 Thessalonians 3:16 Now, may the Lord of peace himself give you peace at all times and in every way.

Hebrews 12:1 - Wherefore seeing we also are compassed about with so great a cloud of witnesses, let us lay aside every weight, and the sin which doth so easily beset us, and let us run with patience the race that is set before us.

Exodus 18:23 - "God will direct you, you will be able to endure."

Galatians 6:9 - "And let us not grow weary of doing good, for in due season we will reap, if we do not give up."

2 Corinthians 4:8 - "We are afflicted in every way, but not crushed; perplexed, but not driven to despair; persecuted, but not forsaken; struck down, but not destroyed."

Romans 12:21 - "Do not be overcome by evil but overcome evil with good."

John 14:15 - "If you love me, you will keep my commandments."

Philippians 4:6-7 – "Be careful for nothing; but in everything by prayer and supplication with thanksgiving let your requests be made known unto God. And the peace of God, which passeth all understanding, shall keep your hearts and minds through Christ Jesus."

Philippians 4:8 – "Finally, brethren, whatsoever things are true, whatsoever things are honest, whatsoever things are just, whatsoever things are pure, whatsoever things are lovely, whatsoever things are of good report; if there be any virtue, and if there be any praise, think on these things."

Romans 12:12 - "Rejoice in hope, be patient in tribulation, be constant in prayer."

Isaiah 40:29 - "He gives power to the faint, and to him who has no might he increases strength."

James 1:12 - "Blessed is the man who remains steadfast under trial, for when he has stood the test he will receive the crown of life, which God has promised to those who love him."

Proverbs 19:21 - "Many are the plans in the mind of a man, but it is the purpose of the LORD that will stand."

Psalm 16:8 - "I have set the LORD always before me; because he is at my right hand, I shall not be shaken."

Matthew 24:13 - "But the one who endures to the end will be saved"

1 Chronicles 16:11 - "Seek the LORD and his strength; seek his presence continually!"

Psalms 6:2 - Have mercy upon me, O LORD; for I am weak: O LORD, heal me; for my bones are vexed.

2 Thessalonians 3:3 The Lord is faithful, who shall stablish you, and keep you from evil.

Jeremiah 32:27 - Behold, I am the LORD, the God of all flesh: is there anything too hard for me?

Isaiah 41:10 - "Do not fear, for I am with you; do not be dismayed, for I am your God. I will strengthen you and help you; I will uphold you with my righteous right hand."

Isaiah 54:5-8 - "'Your Creator will be your husband; the Lord of Heaven's Armies is his name! He is your Redeemer, the Holy One of Israel, the God of all the earth. For the Lord has called you back from your grief—as though you were a young wife abandoned by her husband,' says your God…. 'with everlasting love I will have compassion on you,' says the Lord, your Redeemer."

Psalm 68:5 - "A father to the fatherless, a defender of widows, is God in his holy dwelling."

Philippians 4:13 - "For I can do everything through Christ, who gives me strength."

Philippians 4:19 - "And this same God who takes care of me will supply all your needs from his glorious riches, which have been given to us in Christ Jesus."

Hebrews 13:8 - "Jesus Christ is the same yesterday, today, and forever."

Colossians 1:9-11 – "For this cause we also, since the day we heard it, do not cease to pray for you, and to desire that ye might be filled with the knowledge of his will in all wisdom and spiritual understanding; That ye might walk worthy of the Lord unto all pleasing, being fruitful in every good work, and increasing in the knowledge of God; Strengthened with all might, according to his glorious power, unto all patience and longsuffering with joyfulness."

Psalm 46:1-3 God is our refuge and strength, an ever-present help in trouble. Therefore, we will not fear, though the earth gives way and the mountains fall into the heart of the sea, though its waters roar and foam and the mountains quake with their surging.

Proverbs 18:10 The name of the Lord is a strong tower; the righteous run into it and are safe.

Nehemiah 8:10 Do not grieve, for the joy of the Lord is your strength.

Isaiah 41:10 So do not fear, for I am with you; do not be dismayed, for I am your God. I will strengthen you and help you; I will uphold you with my righteous right hand.

Exodus 15:2 The Lord is my strength and my song; he has given me victory. This is my God, and I will praise him— my father's God, and I will exalt him!

Psalm 9:9-10 The Lord is a refuge for the oppressed, a stronghold in times of trouble.

Psalm 34:10 - Those who seek the Lord lack no good thing.

Isaiah 26: 3-4 Those of steadfast mind you keep in peace—because they trust in you. Trust in the Lord forever, for in the Lord God you have an everlasting rock.

Numbers 6:24-26 - The Lord bless thee and keep thee: The Lord make his face shine upon thee and be gracious unto thee: The Lord lift up his countenance upon thee and give thee peace.

Deuteronomy 6:6-7 - And these words, which I command thee this day, shall be in thine heart: And thou shalt teach them diligently unto thy children, and shalt talk of them when thou sittest in thine house, and when thou walkest by the way, and when thou liest down, and when thou risest up.

John 16:33 - These things I have spoken unto you, that in me ye might have peace. In the world ye shall have tribulation: but be of good cheer; I have overcome the world.

1 Thessalonians 5:16-18 - Rejoice evermore. Pray without ceasing. In everything give thanks: for this is the will of God in Christ Jesus concerning you.

Take a moment to speak these scriptures out loud in your home as often as you think about living a life of abundance. Remind yourself to whom you belong and what He has already accomplished in your life. Then claim—or take—this Word for yourself. Trust that God who began a good work in your life will indeed complete it.

Declare and decree this day that you will win at this opportunity as a single parent. You are a Queen/King that shall live and not die. I do not care what your situation looks like! You will always be the head and never the tail. You will lend and not borrow. Take your rightful place, stand up and face your challenges head on and know that you will succeed at whatever you put forth your hand to do. Develop a "no matter what" attitude and determine within yourself that you will triumph in such a time as this. You are not the first person to face this challenge and you will not be the last. Let me twist this and soften it a bit. Your experience as a single parent should provide you the wisdom and fortitude to provide hope and guidance to any single parent. Your life should be so much of an example that people are inspired just by the very mention of your name. What do you want your legacy to look like? This is what you should focus on when the challenges of being a single parent seem to be too much. The journey will likely be challenging, but nothing worth having is easy. A mother who refused to accept her children living beneath who she gave birth to. I was willing to sacrifice what I wanted to make sure my children had a better life.

I used to tell my sons when it starts to get unbearable think of how much work most famous people had to do to get where they are. Michael Jordan did not make the high school basketball team the first time he tried out and Steve Harvey was homeless at one point during his career. I had to take that same advice as a single parent and let me tell you every time I think of these great people and their stories it would jerk me right out of a pity party and into fifth gear.

I knew if:
- My Auntie who raised four kids by herself after being shot by her ex-husband three times, who is not only surviving but thriving, and is the inspiration and matriarch to our family….then I could too.

- Job, who lost everything (i.e., his children, his good name, his health, his wealth, his wife and his friends) and still could still praise God and remain faithful… then I could too.

- David, who had to wait almost 15 years to become the King he had been anointed and chosen to be… then I could too.

- Moses, who turned to God for help with all his struggles and God protected and delivered Moses… then I could too.

- Joseph, who could forgive and bless his family and those who intentionally schemed to destroy him… then I could too.

- Abraham, who could trust God enough to leave all his family and sacrifice his son he waited years for…then I could too.

- Jacob, who could wrestle with God until God blessed him…then I could too.

- Nehemiah, who could pray, plan and persevere to rebuild the Jerusalem wall… then I could too.

- Esther, who could have courage, uncompromising faith, humility, favor, obedience and loyalty… then I could too.

- Ruth, who could be found by her Boaz and experience the beauty of God's redemptive love… then I could too.

And you can too! The big take away that I hope you glean from my story and the people I interviewed is that when you face challenges, step back and pause (Selah) to reflect on how you made it this far in life. Also, pay attention to how others faced challenges but still reached their destiny. Find strength and motivation through the stories of others and even more importantly through your own successes to thrive even in the midst of adversity. Please know that you are more than enough, and you were designed to handle everything life presents. You were created in God's image to rule and He has commanded you to be strong and of a good courage. You were born with the power to *Be Intentional No Matter What*. It will take a lot of work, but it is possible. If at any point you need support while on this journey we call life, please reach out to me at www.selahinspiration.com.

ACKNOWLEDGEMENTS

When I was eight years old, I lost my father to a horrible accident and as a result I have always been fascinated by people who talked about having a relationship with their father. Having both parents involved in a child's life is a necessity that is highly underestimated in terms of the emotional and psychological development of a child. That is not to say that the child will never reach his or her full potential in life, but oftentimes the child may progress at a slower rate than when both parents are actively involved. Although, I grew up without my father, I had a relatively strong village of people that taught and inspired me to do my best at having the best life possible.

As a result, I am a very determined woman and have faced challenges head on, but when I started going through my divorce I did not want to face the challenge of raising two boys by myself. And it had nothing to do with the effort in raising them but everything to do with not being able to protect them from the hurt they would experience. I understood enough to know that I was going to be okay, but I needed help in reassuring the boys that they were more than the by-product of divorce parents.

So, one night after putting them to bed I really poured out my heart to God. The first prayer was, "Lord, please help us." My second prayer was, "God, I know how to be a Mother to these boys, but I am going to need some help with what Fathers provide for their sons." God met me half-way and sent the provisions we needed to sustain us. It was not easy and at times I was extremely overwhelmed, but I stayed the course. Due to my commitment, God sent people along to help us and it I would be remiss not to acknowledge them.

To my Grandfather, Augustus, who is no longer with us: Thank you for loving on the boys. We needed you here longer, but your short time with them laid a foundation that will never be broken. They smile each time I mention your name.

To my brother PJ who is the ultimate confidant. Thanks for always listening and providing wisdom.

To my Mom for always reminding me that prayer still works and as a result I would come out of any struggle as a better person.

To Derrick, who always expressed concern about us and was willing to help with whatever the children and I needed. We appreciate you. You are very special to us. There are no words that will ever express how fortunate we are to have you in our lives. I love you and I am forever grateful for you.

To my Aunt Jackie and Cousin Star: Words will never be able to express my gratitude of how you extended your home, Motherly care and wisdom to my boys while I traveled for work. I become teary eyed every time I think of how much you cared for them and for me when we had no one else to step up to the plate.

To Pastor Allen who exemplifies the true meaning of stewardship over people: Thank you for popping up at the boy's school to check on them and to let everyone there know that the boys had a well-respected male figure in their lives. I can remember you calling me seven something in the morning on the day I had to attend a parent-teacher conference by myself and saying, "I wish I could be there to support you, but I want you to go in that meeting with your head held high and know that the Lord is with you. You are not alone." I sat through the meeting and listened to a principal and seven teachers give me their story on why they thought my child should be on Ritalin and/or be admitted to a psychiatric clinic for young children. As the second teacher began to speak, I heard, "You are not alone – there is an army standing with you and I promised you when you were sixteen, that I would be there to help you through life. Sit up straight, posture yourself towards each person as they speak, take notes and focus on the eyes of each person as they speak." By the time the third teacher started to talk, the table started to shift and every teacher after that said, "I was called to attend this meeting. Your son does not give me any issues. I have no comment." One white male teacher added to that and said, "Ma'am I applaud you for attending this meeting by yourself and defending your child." He went on to say, "Your son is a pleasure to have in my class and has the typical energy level that any six-year old would have. You just have to address him with firmness." I know it was God's presence in the school and your prayers, that covered us.

To Reverend Brooks, who is a fire and brimstone advocate for all children: My God!!! I still remember the first time I brought them to Mount Pleasant Baptist Church. That morning the boys fought me tooth and nail, because they did not want to visit another church. We finally made it to the church, and they were not happy and made snarly remarks throughout the service until you started preaching. KD was writing about his discontent with the church and when we got home, I decided to read about his experience. To my surprise, the end of his story said, "I did not like anything about this church, but I really like this pastor. He was funny and I could relate to what he was saying." Thank you for showing interest in my young men, being a role model and for constantly pouring into them.

To Cousin Carl who embraced us as his own children: We hold dear to our hearts all the get it together talks, camping trips, holiday dinners, Sunday family dinner and exciting tailgates followed by a football game held at the Washington stadium.

To my Uncle Big Bay and Auntie Dee for encouraging me that I had everything inside me to make a good life for the boys and myself

To the Holoman crew for mentoring and providing tough love to the boys: Thank you for taking me in as their daughter, pouring their wisdom into me and always having my back. The chills when I think about this type of unconditional love.

To Barbara G. and the girls: We have not always seen eye-to-eye but thank you for always being there, ready to fight anyone that came against me and my boys. They still feel the love, and I am forever grateful.

To Jackie W. for always helping me to focus on the bigger picture and get over myself. Thank you for acknowledging my feelings but having enough wisdom to advise me that I need to understand my emotional state is just that but should not dictate my actions.

To my girlfriend, Yolonda D. for always keeping it real: I appreciate you putting my children's wellbeing first while having fun with them all at the same time. From time to time, I would test them in front of other friends and ask them who is Mom's craziest friend and you better know it – after an outburst of laughter they would say, "Ms. Yolonda." We love you and got your back.

To my bestie since grade school Caprissa B.: Thank you for always checking in on me and reminding me that there is nothing like old friends who genuinely want to see you succeed. Thanks for not looking down on me and for always having a heart that knew exactly what to say and exactly how to say it when everything looked impossible. And most importantly, thanks for allowing Nick to share his "nasty" bake beans with me while I was traveling for work, (Inside joke). My brother can cook, and I would love a plate full right now. I am forever grateful for that spread he labored over for me during a very stressful time that made me feel like I had "back home people" supporting me in an unknown place.

To my sister from another Mother Grace G. and family: Thanks for having a listening ear and opening your home to us especially during the holidays. I will forever be grateful for all the memories we created during the weekends and spring break vacations.

To Pastor Graham: Thank you for always taking time to share a simple smile and encourage the boys to be nothing short of great people.

To Reverend Artis: Thank you for taking time to meet and provide counseling as needed.

And last but certainly not least – to all the people who semi-coauthored this book: Thank you for sharing your story through a rather transparent interview about your experience as a single parent.

This type of support empowered me to believe in my ability to raise two boys by myself. It also gave me the wherewith all to buckle down and commit to developing children who understood that I expected greatness from them. I am not saying I was a perfect Mother. Oh, no, by no means, but my deepest intentions were to make sure my children knew I loved them and wanted the best for them. I also understood that as much as I wanted to provide everything for my boys, that I was not completely capable as a woman. There was no way for me to understand what they were going through, as young men. So, I prayed and asked God to send me Godly men who could help them, hence the village of phenomenal men I mentioned above. My mind understood the challenge, but my willingness to receive help created the exact support system I needed. I decided I had to be intentional no matter what I was facing. You see for me, I realized I birthed greatness and I refused to waste that greatness due to a situation I did not create. I wanted my children to believe they came from greatness and they were destined to be great. I am forever grateful for my village and the support they continue to give us. Get yourself a village that has you and your children's best interest in mind.

Even when I did not know how I was going to make it, even when I felt overwhelmed, even when those closest attempted to destroy my character and treat me like I would never amount to anything, I decided I was going to push forward and actively be aware of the energy I allowed to be in my space. I was intentional about what fueled my thoughts and actions. Anything or anyone whose energy was opposite of my goal to create the best life possible for my children and I was put on the back burner. Throughout my journey, I often reminded myself of Winston Churchill's prolific speech given at an Oxford University graduation. The graduates were excited and prepared for a message full of inspirational slogans that would provide enough motivation to push each one to his/her next level. The Dean proudly announced, "It is an honor to have Prime Minister Winston Churchill as our speaker today." Churchill stood up to the applause and cheers; pausing as if to relish the admiration of the students, and in a convincing voice shouted three unforgettable words, "Never give up!" He paused this time as if to take in the significance of the quietness, and very strongly bellowed the words again, "Never give up!" Without another word, Churchill turned sharply, reached for his belongings and slowly walked off, satisfied that he had motivated the graduates. It is really that simple. "Never give up!" Will there be moments that you want to succumb to the barriers and distractions of life or get entangled with drama that does not benefit your ultimate goal. Absolutely! But, resolve within yourself that you will not let anyone, or anything convince you to lose focus. Please do not give in and do not give up.

There is a difference between giving in and giving up. I knew I would never give up, but I had to remind myself to ignore the distractions and challenges that would result in me allowing situations to take precedence over what I needed to focus on to ensure my boys and I had the best life possible. My young men became my "why" in life. My why became my motivation and pushed me to want more than a mediocrity – to want more than just to survive but thrive in the game of live. Everything I did was centered around creating building blocks they could utilize to have the best possible life. It was uncomfortable and challenging, but I made up in my mind, come hell or high water that I was going to persevere through the challenges and hardships and focus on my why.

As a single parent, I had to also ask myself what type of life did I envision for the boys and myself and I made a conscious decision to ignore those who said I would not be able to raise two black boys to become productive, contributing black men. The first thing I did was establish our family values. To me God, family, health, community and joy were all important values that I need to model and ensure my children understood to be important in living our best life.

What I did not realize, early in my single parent journey, was that through every challenge my values allowed my faith to increase and my mindset to elevate at new levels beyond my imagination. During my early years as a single Mom, I cried and worried a lot. Then one day God reminded me that He was with me and was going to help me get through the challenges and overcome the disappointments. As a result, I continued to press forward and through each success story, I realized more and more that the storms were just storms. They did not frighten me but strengthened my will to overcome whatever I was facing. I understood that since the storms would not just disappear that I had to become fiercer and wiser than what I was facing. This concept became a part of me and instead of complaining about what was happening I started keeping a journal of how I overcame each challenge. The notes in my journal included every single detail from the start of a challenge to the end. This help me to visually see how I was thinking and if I was actually taking the right steps, or for that matter, any steps to have the life I was saying I wanted for myself and my children. It also helped me to see all the great things I had done to achieve what we had and to be grateful in that alone.

I was uncomfortable, alone and frustrated at times, but I knew God was going to bring glory to my story, because I was working towards doing what was right. Now, this did not mean I did not doubt God, because, let me tell you, my first thought was, "Why am I having to experience single parenting?" I thought I had done this thing call life, the right way, by getting married and seeking to build a family, but the person who I thought would be there through whatever, surprisingly, decided to abandon, not just me, but his own children. However, I knew that God would not abandon us - to include my ex-husband regardless of his decision. I knew that the storms were happening to build my character and make me a better and stronger person. So, through faith and perseverance I became the perfect storm that refused to allow circumstances, people and challenges to dictate how my life would be lived. I was not going to live a defeated, bitter, victimized life. In fact, I decided through the tears and uncertainty that my sons and I were going to be intentional about living our very best life – no matter what. It was this fundamental mindset that forced me to look beyond the excuses, the stories, the divorce, the hateful people, the negative stuff trying to formulate our identity and commit to fighting for the life I knew my children and I deserved.

References

"Household Relationship and Living Arrangements of Children Under 18 Years". United States Census Bureau. 2015.

(Owens, D. "Recognizing the Needs of Bereaved Children in Palliative Care" Journal of Hospice & Palliative Nursing. 2008; 10:1)

www.pewresearch.org

https://www.pewsocialtrends.org/2018/04/25/the-changing-profile-of-unmarried-parents/

www.singlemotherguide.com/single-mother-statistics

https://www.statista.com/statistics/252847/number-of-children-living-with-a-single-mother-or-single-father/

https://www.wealthysinglemommy.com

https://en.wikipedia.org/wiki/Single_parents_in_the_United_States

About the Author

Toledo Lopez is a Mom, Transformational and Mindset Life Coach, speaker, trainer and former Reading Specialist. Toledo travels around the world sharing her knowledge and expertise through dedicated workshops based on the needs of her clients. She specializes in helping others create a life of confidence and abundance through personal development, coaching and leadership training. Toledo is on a mission to share her wisdom she learned as a single Mom with others to utilize as measurable action in living their best life. Learn more at selahinspiration.com.

Toledo is a graduate of East Carolina University and George Mason University. She received her Master's degree in Leadership and Technology Management. She is the founder and CEO of Selah Inspiration, LLC and a volunteer at local grade-level schools. Toledo lives in Ashburn, Virginia.

Toledo Lopez

Denola M. Burton
DenolaBurton@EnhancedDNA1.com
www.EnhancedDNAPublishing.com

www.ingramcontent.com/pod-product-compliance
Lightning Source LLC
Chambersburg PA
CBHW070156100426
42743CB00013B/2933